Two Blocks
From
Happiness

One Woman's Struggle
for Happiness

by Lois Elliott Morse

STANDARD PUBLISHING
Cincinnati, Ohio   3005

Cover Photo

© 1980 by Robert Cushman Hayes
All Rights Reserved

Library of Congress Cataloging in Publication Data

Morse, Lois Elliott.
    Two blocks from happiness.

      1. Christian life—1960-.   2. Women—Religious
life. 3. Morse, Lois Elliott.   I. Title.
BV4501.2.M592   1985   248.4   84-23934
ISBN 0-87239-860-9

DEDICATION

It was a routine mail. Except for one letter.

With Martha's permission I share these few lines from her ten-page handwritten letter:

"I must share this story because it is devouring me.

"I am a woman (child) 56 years old. I am still looking for my identity. I can't find Martha. Who is she? What is she? Where does she belong? What are her gifts or gift that everyone is supposed to have and be able to give away and share with her loved ones, children, grandchildren, husband, friends (of which I have none). I don't know why. Is it because I am so shallow? Is it because there truly is no me? I am a hodgepodge of many people who raised me to the age of seven. Then I went on my own more or less after I was twelve years old to twenty-one. I am one of eleven children, and I was not wanted. . . .

"I can't remember ever being touched and loved by my parents. My mother told me she never wanted me and did everything she could to get rid of me before I was born. . . .

"I don't suppose if I live to be one hundred I will ever stop crying because I was not loved and wanted. I'm at the age of 56 still searching for a loving mother. . . . I spend days doing nothing. It's as though I'm frozen in place. I cannot function. I don't know how to give of myself. I go to church, but I can't build a Christian relationship with anyone. I just cannot open up and talk and thereby nourish friendship. . . . I was baptized and know the Bible says put away the old self and put on the new, but I continue to flounder around. Can you help me? . . . . I listen, but I don't hear. I see, but am *blind*. I read, but I don't understand. Martha"

This book is dedicated with love to Martha—and to all of the other "Marthas" out there who, for reasons unique to them, seek and have trouble finding.

A fellow struggler and sister in Christ,

Lois Elliott Morse

Contents

A Preview of a Journey

I have been filled with unsteadiness,
possessing enough of God to walk—howbeit,
not without my private canes.

At the close of an autobiography which I penned during my high-school days I wrote, "I wish to devote my life to the work of a missionary. Nothing would give me more satisfaction than serving people in this manner. I have always had a desire to work with poor people who live close to the soil—close to nature (you might say a backward country). Any time I have the pleasure of seeing films of foreign lands I always picture myself working in that field.... Wherever I go, however, I want to be a missionary in some place, at home or foreign, serving and winning people to Christ. This is my life work."

* * * * *

One day after LaVerne and I had come in from boating, the Lord seemed to be saying to me, "Lois, what do you really want?" (I did not hear an actual voice. I am using figurative language throughout this piece of writing.) And I answered, "Lord, I met this handsome young man! I want to marry him and go to the country of Burma to serve You." God said, "My grace is sufficient for you." And I replied, "Lord, I'm so glad You understand! Your grace and LaVerne really are sufficient for me."

On Friday evening, March 27, 1953, the wedding march swelled from the chapel pipe organ, and dressed in satin and lace, I linked my arm in the arm of my father and walked down the aisle of my dreams. In my hand I held a white Bible on top of which lay a white orchid with lily of the valley streamers. Soon LaVerne and I were standing side by side exchanging vows. Then came that long-looked-forward-to moment when we were pronounced "husband and wife."

One spring day of the following year as I was about to head down a flight of stairs, my heel slipped on the landing. I fell flat on my back down the steps. LaVerne arrived just in time to help me back to our apartment. We were both concerned about the little one we were expecting. Later I was rushed to the hospital. The Lord saw me in my pain. He came to me and said, "Lois, what do you really want?" And I cried, "Oh, God, I want our baby!" He answered, "My grace is sufficient for you." I replied, "Oh, Lord, I'm so glad You understand! Your grace and my baby really are sufficient for me." A short time after that the miscarriage was completed.

In November of that same year, 1954, LaVerne and I went to San Francisco on the first leg of our journey to the Orient. After arriving, we walked down to the pier to take a look at the freighter on which we were booked to sail. She was a ten-thousand ton, cream-colored Scandinavian beauty named the *M.S. Peter Maersk.* We loaded our things into cabin number 7 and began to settle in. Shortly after midnight, November 5, we slipped quietly away from the pier and sailed out into the bay. One month later we docked halfway around the world in Bangkok, Thailand.

Since LaVerne had lived in Burma as a missionary previous to our marriage, all of his papers to reenter the country were in order. However, the government had not yet responded to my application for an entry permit. So we decided I should wait behind in Bangkok while LaVerne flew on to Rangoon, the capital of Burma, to make a personal appeal to the government on my behalf. We thought we would be separated only a brief time. I waited and waited and waited. The little one we were expecting grew and grew and grew—week after week, month after month.

One morning about four o'clock or so I awoke from my sleep and shortly found myself in tears. I swung my feet over the side of the bed and continued to weep in an attempt to release the terrible pain of loneliness that lay on my heart. The Lord saw my tears. He came to me and said, "Lois, what do you really want?" I whimpered, "Lord, I can't stay here any longer." And He responded, "My grace is sufficient for you." I answered, "Oh, Lord, I'm so glad You understand! Your grace and a Burmese visa really are sufficient for me." After six months of waiting, I was granted the visa.

Then came long years of laboring together for Christ in northernmost Burma together with LaVerne's beloved family—his parents, Mr. and Mrs. J. Russell Morse, his brother Eugene and wife, Helen, and children, his brother Robert and wife, Betty, and children, and his Chinese-Tibetan foster sister, Drema Esther and her husband, Jesse Yangmi, and children.

During the summer of 1956, over three hundred preachers and prospective preachers from all over the mission field gathered together to attend a six-week Bible school at the Rawang village where we were living. On the evening of August 5, some of the Rawang students from the churches in the northern part of the field came to our home. They wanted to talk with LaVerne about something that was very important. They brought with them a Daru Christian who lived in the far north along the Tibetan border and who had double-staged about fifteen days' journey with the urgent news. When going up into the mountains to hunt for game and dig for medicinal herbs, the runner had found that 3,000 heavily-armed Communist troops had crossed the border onto the Burma side. The troops told him and the other local people that they intended to capture Putao, the government town close to us, within three weeks and that it was useless for anyone to think of resistance or flight.

That night I was afraid. As I was lying in bed, God came to me and said, "Lois, what do you really want?" I answered, "Lord, I want You to send those Communist troops back over the border!" He replied, "My grace is sufficient for you." And I cried, "Oh, Lord, I'm so glad You understand! Your grace and the removal of these Communist troops really are sufficient for me." As the night passed away, so did all of my fears. In time the Communists retreated.

Those were busy years on the field. I did what any other missionary wife and mother would have done. I tried to adjust to my situation, to be a good wife and mother, and to help with the work as I could. My first love in the area of service was in the field of music. I gave many hours of my life teaching the tribal people to sing—a cappella, in four-part harmony, in their own language, and according to their own unique system of music notation. We sang not only simple hymns but learned such difficult music as the "Halle-lujah Chorus," which is incorporated into the Lisu hymnals.

One day while I was waving my arm, the Lord thought it would be a good time to catch me. He came to me and said, "Lois, I see you directing that choir as though you have it all together. But what do you really want?" I replied, "Lord, I'm so homesick!" He said, "My grace is sufficient for you." I answered, "Oh, Lord, I'm so glad You understand! Your grace and a trip home really are sufficient for me." Furlough time finally came around, and we went home.

When we returned to Burma for a second term of service, I was about five months pregnant with our third child. We planned for her to be born in our grass-roofed home in Muladi village. I went into labor about four-thirty Sunday afternoon, October 2, 1960. Immediately we began to pre-pare for the baby's arrival. LaVerne and Drema were with me. The tractor and driver were finally rounded up and left for Putao to fetch the doctor—a trip of about nine miles through the grasslands. The minutes ticked slowly away into hours. My contractions were coming one, two, and three minutes apart. About eight forty-five, Dr. Zau Hkawng and Betty, Robert's wife, arrived by jeep. Around ten thirty, I let out a cry, that must have reached Thailand, as Cindy was ready to be fully delivered. The Lord heard my cry. He came to me and said, "Lois, what do you really want?" I groaned, "Lord, I could really use a little something for the pain right now!" He replied, "Hang in there, Lois! My grace is sufficient for you." And I answered, "Oh, Lord, I'm so glad You under-stand! Your grace and a whiff of gas really are sufficient for me." Just then Betty spoke to me ever so lovingly and sup-portively. Her words were more helpful than any whiff of gas I've ever received! In a moment, Cindy was born. Betty had been writing down my contractions. At ten thirty-five, she wrote, "Hooray! A girl!"

As time went on, I thought I could be so much happier if we could only serve the Lord someplace else. In my mind I boarded a ship as did Jonah.[1] I climbed down into the hold of the ship and fell asleep. And the Lord found me there. He nudged me and said, "Lois, what are you doing down here?

What do you really want?" I answered, "It's too hard, Lord! Please give us another ministry." He replied, "My grace is sufficient for you." And I cried, "Oh, Lord, I'm so glad You understand! Your grace and a new field of service really are sufficient for me." We stayed right where we were.

We returned to the States after our second term on the mission field and lived in a little two-bedroom house in Cincinnati, Ohio. We had purchased it when we had two small children. Now we were a family of seven! One day the Lord came to me and said, "Lois, what do you really want?" I responded, "Lord, I want a home I can really love that meets my needs and the needs of the whole family." He answered, "My grace is sufficient for you." And I replied, "Lord, I sure am glad You're going to do something about this! Your grace and another home really are sufficient for me." Years later the home was granted in God's own time and in God's own way.

During the years that followed there were all kinds of problems going on in one part of my world. I poured out my heart with advice, and when it wasn't heeded, I felt like Ahithophel who, when he saw his counsel wasn't followed, saddled his donkey, went to his city, put his household in order, and hanged himself![2] The Lord came to me and said, "Lois, what do you really want?" I replied, "Lord, You've got to take care of these problems!" He responded, "My grace is sufficient for you." And I answered, "Oh, Lord, I'm so glad You understand! Your grace and the removal of these problems really are sufficient for me." Years later, they were resolved.

Then one day I sat down under a juniper tree like Elijah and prayed that I might die even as he prayed.[3] While I was sitting there thinking, the Lord came to me and said, "Lois, what do you really want?" I answered, "I just want to die, Lord!" He replied, "My grace is sufficient for you." And I responded, "Oh, Lord, I'm so glad You understand! Your grace and an exit from this world really are sufficient for me." I kept on living.

Time went by, and the Lord wanted to know how things were going with me. He came to me and said, "Lois, what do you really want?" I responded, "You, Lord!" Tears of joy flooded His eyes! Penetrating my gaze, He said, "My grace is sufficient for you." And I answered, "I know, Lord!"[4]

11

[1]Jonah 1:3.

[2]2 Samuel 17:23.

[3]1 Kings 19:4.

[4]Articles written by the author and published first by the Restoration Herald, Cincinnati, Ohio, are quoted in this book on pages 7-11, 19, 20, 25, 26, 32-34, 37-40, 41-42, 50-55, 57-66, 67-75, 77-79, 87-102, 131-134, 141-143, 154-160, 169-172. Used by permission.

Scriptures quoted throughout this book are from the King James Version unless otherwise indicated.

Scripture quotations throughout this book marked NAS are taken from the New American Standard Bible, ©The Lockman Foundation, 1960, 1962, 1963, 1968, 1971, 1973, 1975, 1977. Used by permission.

The Journey Begins

Suddenly Uncle Henry stood up.

"There's a cyclone coming, Em," he called to his wife. "I'll go look after the stock." Then he ran toward the sheds where the cows and horses were kept.

Aunt Em dropped her work and came to the door. One glance told her of the danger close at hand.

"Quick, Dorothy!" she screamed. "Run for the cellar!"

Toto jumped out of Dorothy's arms and hid under the bed, and the girl started to get him. Aunt Em, badly frightened, threw open the trap door in the floor and climbed down the ladder into the small, dark hole. Dorothy caught Toto at last, and started to follow her aunt. When she was halfway across the room there came a great shriek from the wind, and the house shook so hard that she lost her footing and sat down suddenly upon the floor.

A strange thing then happened.

The house whirled around two or three times and rose slowly through the air. Dorothy felt as if she were going up in a balloon. . . .

Toto did not like it. He ran about the room, now here, now there, barking loudly; but Dorothy sat quite still on the floor and waited to see what would happen. . . .

Hour after hour passed away, and slowly Dorothy got over her fright; but she felt quite lonely, and the wind shrieked so loudly all about her that she nearly became deaf. . . . At last she crawled over the swaying floor to her bed, and lay down upon it; and Toto followed and lay down beside her.

In spite of the swaying of the house and the wailing of the wind, Dorothy soon closed her eyes and fell fast asleep.[1]

* * * * *

As you and I travel to our heavenly home, we find ourselves in much the same predicament as Dorothy in the fairy tale, *The*

Wizard of Oz. We were driven out of our original home, the garden of Eden, and are wandering about in another land as strangers and exiles.[2] We're traveling on the road that leads to the throne of God so that God can help us find our way home again. Our enemy is Satan. Our companions are three: the Scarecrow, the Tin Woodman, and the Lion.

Part of the secret of finding our way on the road that leads to the city of God lies in making friends with our companions, in being sympathetic with their misfortunes and struggles, and in caring for their deepest needs.

I invite you to travel with me on a journey that may change your life. Listen carefully to the Scarecrow, the Tin Woodman, and the Lion. As you identify with their heart cries and problems, you may come to an understanding of yourself.

---

[1]L. Frank Baum, *The Wizard of Oz* (New York: The Macmillan Company), pp. 13, 17-18, 45-46, 109-110, 173-174.

[2]Hebrews 11:13.

Part One

Develop Your Mind

Make Friends With
Your Mind

"Who are you?" asked the Scarecrow, when he had stretched himself and yawned. "And where are you going?"

"My name is Dorothy," said the girl, "and I am going to the Emerald City, to ask the great Oz to send me back to Kansas."

"Where is the Emerald City?" he inquired. "And who is Oz?"

"Why, don't you know?" she returned in surprise.

"No, indeed; I don't know anything. You see, I am stuffed, so I have no brains at all," he answered sadly.

"Oh," said Dorothy; "I'm awfully sorry for you."

"Do you think," he asked, "if I go to the Emerald City with you, that the great Oz would give me some brains?"

"I cannot tell," she returned. "but you may come with me, if you like. If Oz will not give you any brains you will be no worse off than you are now."

"That is true," said the Scarecrow. "You see," he continued, confidentially, "I don't mind my legs and arms and body being stuffed, because I cannot get hurt. If anyone treads on my toes or sticks a pin into me, it doesn't matter, for I can't feel it. But I do not want people to call me a fool, and if my head stays stuffed with straw instead of with brains, as yours is, how am I ever to know anything?"

"I understand how you feel," said the little girl, who was truly sorry for him. "If you will come with me I'll ask Oz to do all he can for you."

"Thank you," he answered gratefully.

They walked back to the road, Dorothy helped him over the fence, and they started along the path of yellow brick for the Emerald City. . . .

At noon Dorothy and the Scarecrow sat beside the roadside, near a little brook. Dorothy opened her basket and took out some

17

bread. She offered a portion of the bread to the Scarecrow, but he refused.

"I am never hungry," he said. "And it is a lucky thing I am not. For my mouth is only painted, and if I should cut a hole in it so I could eat, the straw I am stuffed with would come out, and that would spoil the shape of my head."

* * * * *

We all know what it's like to have our heads stuffed with straw and to have no appetite for God. We've crawled out of bed in the morning, stumbled over our Bibles, and reached for our spiritual cosmetic cases. Then we've stood in front of our mirrors, painted on our spiritual mouths, and gone out the front door with the shape of our heads still intact.

Because the Word of God, unlike any other book, is God-breathed, we cannot read it and remain the same. I believe it is not so much lack of time as it is the presence of fear, anger, or guilt which keeps us from the Word. We simply don't enjoy being around someone who evokes these feelings in us—even when that someone is God.

Sometimes we're afraid of God. We simply don't understand His nature or His dealings with us, and we want to run away. I'm reminded of a note our son Mark wrote when he was just a little boy:

"to Mommy Sear Mother I ran away because you wont give me $50 Dollars. Tonight I will come back if there is not $50 Dollars on my bed I will go away for a week and when I come back if there is not $50 on my bed I will stay away till the school stadts. I have my sleeping mattress and covers and my p. j. s and my swimmig soot and my clocthes. And my sunday shirt and pand and tie. Love Mark Morse"

Like Mark, sometimes we feel like running away. We gather our sleeping mattresses, covers, pj's, swimming suits, and clothes—and, of course, our Sunday outfits so we can continue to go to church! But all the same, we're running away from God and His Word.

Sometimes we're angry with God, and we feel like fighting back. I'm reminded of the Christmas convention that was held in our village of Muladi, Burma, back in 1962. There were about four thousand in attendance. Straw was placed over the dirt floor of the church building, and folks were seated on it—the men on one side, the women on the other according to their tribal custom. Messages were given in both the Lisu and Rawang languages with the aid of an interpreter for each message. As you can imagine, the services were not short and sweet as we have them here at home. One of the missionaries was asked to preach at the first service which began in the morning. He preached on and on and on! His wife kept an eye on her watch, and we exchanged understanding glances. Finally, after one o'clock in the afternoon, he brought his message to a close. As he did so, he encouraged the people to abandon any angry feelings that they might have one toward another. When he sat down, his wife said teasingly, "We weren't angry with anyone until you preached so long!"

Sometimes we feel like God just keeps on talking and talking, and we have to sit there in our seats and listen. The hands of the clock keep going around—people don't change, and circumstances don't change. We start to get angry! We simply don't understand God's nature or His dealings with us. And we don't want to spend time with Him or time in His Word.

Other times we're filled with guilt, but we just can't come to God and feed on His Word because that makes us feel guiltier still. Sometimes it's because we confuse how people have treated us with how God is, or how we *think* he is. I remember crying out in pain:

> Lord,
>   why does she use pastels
>   to color her sins—
>   and then color mine BLACK?

> I mean,
>   I know that mine **ARE** black!
>   And I really don't mind her coloring in my book.
>   (We used to swap books when we were kids.)

> It's just that
>   when she shows me her book
>   all done up in the most delicate hues—
>   blues,
>   greens,
>   pinks—

19

I feel so ashamed of myself
I want to hide my book—
                and never let her see
                one page!

Come to think of it, Lord—
    I thought black was the only color for sin
    You said we could use!

        ... I wonder where she got her crayons?

Because we haven't been accepted by people, we think God won't accept us either. We simply don't understand His nature or His dealings with us. So we hide our book, and we hide His book. We don't want to have anything to do with Him.

When we are so filled with fear, anger, or guilt that we can't come to God, we need to see God as He *really* is. Unfortunately, a deeply sensitive woman who has been abused in life may have a tendency to focus in on passages in the Bible that are directed to the rebellious, and therefore receive a distorted view of God. Like Mary Magdalene in the garden scene following Christ's resurrection, she sees Jesus through her veil of tears and supposes Him to be the gardener. What she needs to do is to feed on such passages as the hundred and third Psalm:

> The Lord is compassionate and gracious,
> Slow to anger and abounding in lovingkindness.
> He will not always strive with us;
> Nor will He keep His anger forever.
> He has not dealt with us according to our sins,
> Nor rewarded us according to our iniquities.
> For high as the heavens are above the earth,
> So great is His lovingkindness toward those who fear
>   Him.
> As far as the east is from the west,
> So far has He removed our transgressions from us.
> Just as a father has compassion on his children,
> So the Lord has compassion on those who fear Him.
> For He Himself knows our frame;
> He is mindful that we are but dust.
>   (Psalm 103:8-14, NAS)

A woman who is bound by fear, anger, or guilt suffers from

a disorder that is similar in some ways to anorexia nervosa. *The American Medical Association Family Medical Guide* defines the latter disorder as, "Anorexia nervosa is a refusal to eat that can lead to extreme loss of weight, hormonal disturbances, and even death.... Even after dieting to the point where she is extremely thin, a girl with anorexia nervosa still sees herself as overweight.... Although many parents assume that this disorder is a phase of adolescence, there is often an underlying psychological problem that must be resolved."[1]

A woman suffering from spiritual anorexia nervosa is unable, psychologically, to feed on the Word. She cannot handle anything that would threaten her poor self-image. Harboring a poor understanding of God's nature and of her own nature, she responds to the Bible in much the same way the Scarecrow responded to Dorothy when she offered him some bread from her basket, "I am never hungry."

She is also unable, psychologically, to enter into a deep personal relationship with God. She sees Him as a consuming fire without understanding His full nature, and avoids contact. To her it would be a life-threatening situation. With the Scarecrow she says, "There is only one thing in the world I am afraid of ... a lighted match."

She is also unable, psychologically, to trust. Like the Scarecrow she is raised above God by means of a pole of self-sufficiency. As long as that pole is there, she steels herself against leaning. Her plight is much the same as the plight of the Scarecrow when he said to Dorothy, "I did not like to be deserted this way ... but my feet would not touch the ground, and I was forced to stay on that pole. It was a lonely life to lead ...." Mistaking her self-sufficiency for spiritual strength, she feigns a wholeness she does not possess.

Countless women suffer from spiritual anorexia nervosa to varying degrees of intensity. The beginning of healing comes when a woman, suffering from this disorder, experiences the unconditional love of God in and through others in sufficient amounts and over a sufficient period of time till she becomes hungry for a personal relationship with God and His Word.

To every woman suffering from spiritual anorexia nervosa God stretches out His arms of love and cries:

Ho, every one that thirsteth, come ye to the waters, and he that hath no money; come ye, buy, and eat; yea, come, buy wine and milk without money and without price.

Wherefore do ye spend money for that which is not bread? and your labor for that which satisfieth not? hearken diligently unto me, and eat ye that which is good, and let your soul delight itself in fatness.

(Isaiah 55:1, 2)

There's a Scarecrow inside of you who is traveling with you on the road that leads to the city of God. Make friends with your mind. Sit down with it, and encourage it to talk to God. Then take it by the hand and let it feed day and night on the Word until every piece of "straw" is replaced by the nourishing words of your heavenly Father.

---

[1]Jeffrey R.M. Kunz, MD, Editor-in-Chief, *The American Medical Association Family Medical Guide* (New York: Random House, Inc., 1982), pp. 710, 711.

Make Friends With

God's Word

An evangelist of the Lisu tribe of Burma was so hungry for the Word of God that when he received his first copy of the Bible translated into his own language, he sat down and wrote a psalm of great joy. His letter was addressed to Mr. and Mrs. Allan Crane of the Overseas Missionary Fellowship. Mr. Crane was one of the principal translators of the Bible into the Lisu language. The letter was written from the village of Goomoo, October 6, 1968:

"Hallelujah! Praise and thanks be to God our Father! Although He is high and great, He loves and pities us men of dust, and He has given us our Saviour. Not only so, but that He may have fellowship with us men of earth and might be able to instruct us, He has given us His very precious and great Holy Book. Thanks be to Him.

"That which we have mourned for with tears and longing, hoping and praying, God has granted. On the evening of October 4, my own eyes saw and my own hands held His Holy Word. Hallelujah! Thanks be to God for ever and ever. My heart is filled with joy. My mouth is filled with song. My eyes are filled with gladness. My whole being is filled with satisfaction.

"Everyone who heard the news came running to my house. Whey they saw, they jumped up and clapped their hands. So filled with abounding joy were we all that we literally jumped and hopped around, because we had received what we had longed to see and longed to touch. Thanks again to God our Father, and thanks to you our teachers.

"This is the most precious thing upon this globe. Even if someone would offer me in exchange a thousand kingdoms like this whole wide world, I would never accept and never exchange.

"Teacher, on the fourth of October, during the day, I wrote you a letter—but as I was returning home from a meeting in Myitkyina, I heard the news. I was so happy I ran all the way home and hastily opened the package and just gazed. That night I could not sleep.... Long before daylight I was up reading, and this morning too I was up at first cockcrow reading and reading. Before the fourth evening of October, 1969 arrives I want to read through God's Word completely.

> Yours rejoicing,
> Lucius"[1]

Oh, that we might be as excited as Lucius about the opportunities we have to read and learn from God's Word. God wants us to fill our minds with the knowledge of His Word and apply its truths in our daily lives. Like Lucius, let us hastily open our Bibles, read them with zeal, and make friends with God's Word.

---

[1]*East Asia Millions,* January 1969, p. 9.

Make Friends With

God

The early dew of morning bathed our feet as we crossed the meadow grass together—my thoughts and I. They skipped along beside me like little children—one holding my hand tightly, another darting through the grass to chase a butterfly, and still another dancing ahead of me in her eagerness to arrive at the spot where we met God every day.

When we reached the place of prayer, we sat down amidst the meadow flowers—one in heart, mind, and soul as we bowed in silence before our Creator.

Then one thought lifted up her voice and praised God for His blessings, while another darted across the meadow grass to chase a butterfly of desire, and still another danced ahead, eager to find and do the work of God.

I was distressed in my spirit and said, "Come now, this must never be. Let us gather together to worship the Lord!" My thoughts listened to my voice. Once again we sat hand in hand, with every head bowed, and worshiped God. During those moments the love and grace of God came dancing down the sunbeams till the very light of God was upon us.

In a moment, one of my thoughts, which could never sit still for long, was off to chase a butterfly. Still another hastened off into the fields to get a drink from an earthly spring. Another was caught, held by the love of God, and remained very close to me. This time the love and grace of God poured over my soul and over every divergent thought like a mighty cataract. Suddenly, butterflies and cool drinks from the earthly spring lost their hold. We sat in stillness. In the quietness we worshiped. Then we arose to begin the day's labors, refreshed.

As I crossed the meadow grass, with my thoughts skipping along beside me like little children, I said, "Oh, God, please send Your love and grace into my inmost being, and bring 'every thought captive to the obedience of Christ' (2 Corinthians 10:5, NAS). Then, and only then, let my thoughts loose to skip and dance through the meadow grass of life. Then shall they be so filled with the fragrance of Christ they will no longer need to chase butterflies. For butterflies will come and light upon them! So filled shall they be of living water that they will no longer need to run to earthly springs, for within them will flow streams of mercy never ceasing!"

This time, as my thoughts and I crossed the meadow grass, love, joy, peace, patience, kindness, goodness, faithfulness, gentleness, and self-control covered the meadow flowers as the early dew of morning. Passers-by stopped to pick the spiritual harvest. Together, with the sunbeams, we skipped and danced across the meadow grass of life in the light of the love of God.

I heard a voice behind me crying, "Hallelujah!" And all of my thoughts threw back their heads and laughed with holy laughter!

Hallelujah! And Amen!

We Really Do Need God

Did you ever sing the song, "He Is All I Need"? That can be kind of scary theology because He's up there, and we're down here! We can't touch His hand or look into His face like we can hold each other's hands and look into each other's faces—and that's scary! But we need to remember that the psalmist didn't say, "The Lord is my shepherd; I shall not need." He said, "The Lord is my shepherd; I shall not want" (Psalm 23:1). Why? Because all my needs shall be supplied! There will be water to quench my thirst, bread to satisfy my hunger, hugs to fill my aching loneliness, special blessings to minister to my special needs, hard work to do, things to suffer, and mountains to climb! Since God supplies all of our needs, and far more than this, He really is all we need.

When I went into St. George Hospital as an outpatient to have a tumor removed (It was on my left side just under my ribs—I knew you'd be wondering about that, so I thought I'd tell you!), I saw a card. It was on one of the locker doors where we surgical patients were supposed to hang our belongings before donning booties to cover our shoes, a "shower cap" to cover our hair, and a drab piece of cloth with armholes and snaps down the back—hopefully, to cover us!

Now this card made my day! It simply said,

> "Incredible as it seems,
> my life is based on a true story."

That really struck my funny bone! I liked the author's humor! If I had seen him coming down the street, I would have liked to have stopped long enough to shake hands with him and say, "Thanks for the chuckle you gave me the day I had surgery."

I wish I could write a book for you about the totally victorious, fascinating, and inspiring story of my life—as I wish I had lived it! It would be the kind of book you wouldn't be able to put down until 5:00 A.M.--when you would finally snap off the bed lamp and content yourself with one hour of sleep before the alarm went off! But I can't do that because my life is based on a true story. Since I want to be honest with you, I'll have to share myself with you as I really am—not as I wish I had been. Now I hope that doesn't mean you'll snuggle in bed, prop your pillows just so, read for a few minutes, yawn deeply, and drop off to sleep before you can even reach for the bed lamp. Because I have something I want to say to you.

Back in November of 1954, my husband LaVerne and I boarded a freighter and headed in the direction of a primitive tribal village located about seventy air miles south of Tibet, seventy-seven air miles west of Communist China, and twenty air miles east of Assam, India.

One month later we disembarked at Bangkok, Thailand. It was only a short distance by plane from there to Rangoon, Burma. However, we were unable to proceed together as the Burmese government had not yet responded to my application for an entry permit. Since LaVerne had lived in Burma previous to our marriage—laboring there for the Lord along with his parents and other members of his family—all of his papers to reenter the country were in order. So we decided the best thing for us to do under the circumstances was for me to wait behind in Bangkok. I stayed at the Christian Missionary Alliance Guest House while LaVerne flew on to Rangoon to make a personal appeal to the government on my behalf. We thought we would be separated only a short time.

I waited. In February I broke the news to my family back home that we were expecting a bundle from heaven! I waited. March the thirtieth rolled around, and I celebrated my twenty-second birthday. I waited. In April, I wrote these lines to loved ones back home:

"Well, another day has gone by here in Bangkok. Some days go quickly; others drag slowly, hour by hour. Last night around four o'clock or so I awoke from my sleep and shortly found myself in tears. Before long I sat up with my feet dangling over the side of the bed and continued to weep in an attempt to release the terrible pain of loneliness that lay on my heart. All was quiet in the house with the exception of the noise of my fan. Without, I could hear the crickets and every now and then the crow of a rooster not far from the house. I looked through the screened-in windows and sat gazing at the sky and the trees about the compound. There was one lonely star in view. I looked up into the heavens with, I suppose, much the same expression that a child would have who was about to ask a petition of his parents and said, 'Oh God, I can't stay here any longer.' Even as the tears streamed down my cheeks I could sense the triumphant look on Satan's face and imagine his pointing to God and saying, 'See, she can't stick it out.' I rebuked him mentally and said, 'I can too stick it out!' I thought of the words that had come to my mind several times—'Pray not that trials be ended; rather, pray for strength. . . .' As the tears continued to flow I looked again to the heavens and asked God to send His strength down upon me and to forgive me. I began to feel rather weary after a time and lay down again on my pillow and soon went off to sleep."

I do not come to you in great strength—ready to go out and conquer the world for Christ with a bold arm! I come to you in my weakness—sometimes hanging by a thread. What I want to say to you is this: You need more than I am able to give you, and I need more than you are able to give me. You

28

see, if we don't understand this way down deep in our hearts, we just might miss Him and all of the things only He can give—even though we may relate beautifully to each other.

Our need is for God. We really do need Him for our salvation, for our sanctification, for our self-acceptance, and for filling our needs.

We Need God for Our Salvation

The night in which He was betrayed, Jesus said to His disciples, "Let not your heart be troubled. You are trusting God, now trust in me. There are many homes up there where my Father lives, and I am going to prepare them for your coming. When everything is ready, then I will come and get you, so that you can always be with me where I am. If this weren't so, I would tell you plainly" (John 14:1-3, The Living Bible).

Jesus put this promise in a nutshell a little later when He said, "For I will live again—and you will too" (John 14:19, The Living Bible).

Now man has released a lot of power in this world and done a lot of unbelievable things. Rocket fuel can propel a rocket into space, and keep it maneuvering up there for a time. But only God can reach down inside my grave, propel me into space, and keep me maneuvering forever!

Don't misunderstand me! I need you! Oh, do I ever need you. But all of
your love, caring, and strength is not sufficient to take me out of the grave. All of my love, caring, and strength is not sufficient to take you out of the grave.

We really do need God!

* * * * *

Why did You have to die, Lord? Why couldn't You have saved us some other way? Why was the shedding of blood necessary? Some think that only an angry, vengeful God would require such a sacrifice for sin.

Lord, I never mentioned it to You before, but did You know that I agreed with Pilate? He thought You were innocent. He even said to the chief priests and the multitudes, "I find no guilt in this man" (Luke 23:4, NAS). Oh, I wish I had been there.

29

I can see Pilate with an outstretched arm trying to reason with the crowd, "You brought this man to me as one who incites the people to rebellion, and behold, having examined Him before you, I have found no guilt in this man regarding the charges which you make against Him. No, nor had Herod, for he sent Him back to us; and behold, nothing deserving death has been done by Him" (Luke 23:14, 15, NAS). Oh, I would have cried out, "It's true! What Pilate says is true! There is no cause for death in this man." Like Pilate, I would have believed You innocent of all charges, though those around me voiced their accusations. I would have taken my stand.

I remember Pilate saying something about punishing You and then releasing You. Oh, yes, Lord, I agreed with Pilate about that, too. Really, I was so upset that so many wanted to kill You, I didn't even know what I was doing. I was siding with Pilate, and I wanted to get on with the job so You could be set free.

While You were bent over, tied to a post, I picked up the lash of bitterness and applied the blow to Your bare back.

Then I entertained hatred for my brother who wounded me and turned and hurled the lash at You.

Then I fell into judgment over another who irritated me, and again, brought another blow upon Your back.

The sight of blood streaming did not stir me. After all, I had my rights. I criticized one of Your servants and struck another blow.

While You stood there, speechless, I coveted my neighbor's blessing, despised him for what he had, and hurled still another lash at Your back—this time ripping it wide open.

Then I allowed something in my life to become so important to me that You stood by, hurting, in second place. I applied still another lash to your quivering flesh, now covered with blood, but the sight did not move me.

Father, why did You have to die? I believe in You. I am a woman of indomitable faith. No one can accuse You of anything without my fever rising. I plainly declare to all within my hearing that You are innocent of all charges.

Why did You have to die, Lord? Why did You have to die? Why did you have to die?

* * * * *

After the flood God said, "I will never again curse the ground on account of man, for the intent of man's heart is evil from his youth; and I will never again destroy every living thing, as I have done" (Genesis 8:21, NAS). In one of the most heart-rending, powerful statements of Scripture, God said, "It's hopeless." Cursing the ground or destroying the world, the most violent things that could happen, would not be sufficient to gain man's attention or to change him. No catastrophe could break the hardness of hearts touched by sin, nor could anything else—not all of God's dealings with men, not even His coming to earth, not even His miracles, not even His sinless life, not even His pain inflicted from our repeated lashings. He knew He would simply have to come and die—and let men stare in disbelief at His love.

> I can almost see the pain upon His face
> as He stumbles up the hill that He must face.
> There are broken hearts that stare in disbelief.
> You just can't die.
> But thru His tears He smiles.
> "Don't cry for Me. It's almost done.
> It's just what I've longed to do.
> Don't cry for Me. There is no pain
> as great as my love for you."
>
> If they'd only known the miracle within;
> tho' they did not see,
> they watched Him take their sin.
> Precious Son of God,
> how can it end this way?
> It just can't be.
> But as He dies, He breathes,
> "Don't cry for Me. It's almost done.
> It's just what I've longed to do.
> Don't cry for Me. There is no pain
> as great as my love for you."

God's Tears

God said,
"Look down there, Jesus.
Look at the men we've created!
There's nothing in their hearts
but evil day and night."
This was in the days of Noah.
And God was patient
for a hundred and twenty years.
But when those years were finished,
tears flooded God's eyes.
And His tears became a deluge
that covered the whole earth.
Men saw it raining,
but I saw God's tears coming down.

Scene Two

And God said,
"Look down there now, Jesus.
See that ark bobbing on the waters?
I've got a man in there
whose heart is pure.
With him we'll start this world
all over again!"
And after God stopped crying
and the waters abated
from off the face of the earth
God spoke to Noah and said,
"Noah, I promise you
I won't cry anymore as I did
when I told you
to get inside the ark."
And with a gesture of His hand
He swept a rainbow into being.
And every time Noah saw one
up in the sky after a storm,
He remembered God's promise.

Scene Three

Then men turned bad again.
And God wanted to cry.
But He remembered
His promise to Noah.
"Jesus," He said softly,
"it's time now for You
to go down to earth
because there's so much evil
down there day and night."
So Jesus came to earth.
And God cried through Jesus
as He hung on the cross.
When a soldier pierced His side,
men saw blood and water streaming.
But I saw God's tears coming down.
Then Jesus arose
and went back to Heaven.

Scene Four

Once again God looked down
upon the earth.
And there was so much evil
down there day and night.
And God said,
"Jesus, it's time now
to go back down to earth
to gather all of our children.
For my patience is ended,
and I can't cry as I did
when my tears covered the earth.
I promised Noah I wouldn't."

Scene Five

So Jesus came to earth
and took all who loved and followed Him
up to Heaven to be with God.
And for all of God's children
going to Heaven was like seeing

ten million rainbows
after the storm of life.
And it was only
the first day of forever!
And God wiped all their tears away.
Then, after He finished wiping
the eyes of all of His children,
He turned from them for a moment
and wiped the tears of thousands of years
from His own eyes.
And all the tears of God
were locked up forever in hell.
The devil and his angels
and all who followed them
saw it raining fire and brimstone,
but I saw God's tears coming down.
And those who were down there in hell
had to live with that!

Scene Six

But up in Heaven
God said,
"Children, we're not going to cry
anymore!
At that moment
all of the rainbows
that God had stored up in Heaven
fell in line
and formed a path
that led to the throne of God.
That was the first day
I ever walked on a rainbow!
And it was as solid beneath me
as the promises of God.

We Need God for Our Sanctification

Paul said to the Christians at Ephesus, "I pray that you will begin to understand how incredibly great his power is to help those who believe him. It is that same mighty power that raised Christ from the dead and seated him in the place of honor at God's right hand in heaven" (Ephesians 1:19, 20, The Living Bible).

This means that God is not only going to reach down inside my grave, propel me into space, and keep me maneuvering forever, but that same power is working in me today freeing me from the things that bind me, shackle me, and keep me cowering behind the prison bars of my soul!

Now I need you to help unbind me, to help unfasten the shackles that enslave me, to help unlock the prison doors that confine me to my own private hells. But without the power of God working in my life and breaking the power that sin has over me, all of your efforts would be like placing an inch-wide Band-Aid over a twelve-inch gash. It just can't do the job!

We all have deep tears inside our souls that need to be sewn up with God's power before the surgical dressings are applied—or we'll come apart! Maybe that's why some of us remain in bondage for so long. We have Band-Aids and surgical dressings all over us (sometimes!), but we're missing the power of God! Our insides are hanging out. Our Band-Aids are dangling. Our dressings are falling off because it's too much for them to handle.

We really do need God.

We Need God for Our Self-Acceptance

After Adam and Eve ate the forbidden fruit, they sewed fig leaves together and made for themselves loin coverings. When they heard the sound of the Lord God walking in the garden in the cool of the day, they hid themselves.

We invent so many ways of hiding—from ourselves, from others. Sometimes we slide through our lives saying to each other, "We should be very careful that we do not become.... We must not allow ourselves to be.... We must be extra careful to avoid.... Forgive me (in general) wherein I have failed." When what we badly need to be saying is, "I was angry! ... I was wrong in that! ... I want to release both

35

myself and you by telling you that I am not bitter anymore!"

The way we slide around our faults—telling each other what we *should be* instead of confessing what we *are* so we don't have to come to grips with ourselves—might be amusing in a comedy. But it's tragic in real life. It altogether misses the point of the Christian experience! The point of the Christian experience is not to save *our* faces, but to "save" God's face. We need to clearly state to one another and to the world that these negative things in us, that we can't really hide, *are not* Christ manifested in us but our own sinfulness.

When I was in Bangkok waiting for the Burmese government to grant me an entry visa, I did some reading in a book entitled, *British North Borneo,* written by Owen Rutter. Tucked away in its pages was the story of an old Dunsan chief who was lying on his death bed. After the chief had received the Sacrament, the priest leaned over him and asked him if he had any enemies to forgive. "No, Father," he replied. "I have killed them all!"

I don't often hear that kind of honesty from people who profess Christ. And Christ is "losing face" because people are attributing to Him what really belongs in the area of confession. They're all mixed up about what He's really like, and they can't trust Him because *we're* not coming clean.

There are many reasons why we hedge around our sins. Fear of rejection must head the list. It's hard to be rejected.

> I cried out to you,
> but you did not hear me.
>   I bared my soul to you,
>   but you did not clothe it with
>   your love,
>   your understanding,
>   your acceptance.
> I stood in the middle of the
> thoroughfare of life—
>   naked,
>   lonely,
>   cold,
>   forsaken.
> I prayed.
> You paused and looked back at me
>   standing there.
> I waited!

The neat thing is that with God there is no waiting—**NO WAITING!** He loves us just as we are. He stands ready to forgive, to heal, and to uplift.

Don't misunderstand me! I need your forgiveness and acceptance! Oh, do I ever need your forgiveness and acceptance. And you need mine. But without God's forgiveness and acceptance we'd all have to go into hiding. For *He* is the ground of our self-acceptance. With all of that going for us we can have the courage to be honest no matter what our brother thinks. We really do need God!

We Need God for Filling Our Needs

Paul said to the Christians in Philippi, "And it is he who will supply all your needs from his riches in glory, because of what Christ Jesus has done for us" (Philippians 4:19, The Living Bible). David said, "Be delighted with the Lord. Then he will give you all your heart's desires" (Psalm 37:4, The Living Bible).

We can live lives that are radiant with hope, faith, and love because God meets all of our needs and considers all of our desires.

I want to tell you about the biggest fish story you've ever heard. It happened in the middle of a suburb filled with typical suburban homes and loads of cement sidewalks and streets—far from any body of water.

It was time to pay our house taxes, and to be honest with you, we needed a fish! I mean, if the Lord could tell Peter to go get a fish and open its mouth and take out the tax money, why couldn't He do that for us?[1]

One night I was busy in the kitchen, and LaVerne was mumbling something from the black recliner in the family room. Our two youngest, Shirley and Beth, ages thirteen and fourteen, were there. I didn't understand what LaVerne was saying—but the kids yelled, "Mom, you got your fish!" I still wasn't getting the point, and LaVerne couldn't figure our what on earth they were talking about. He didn't know about my fishing plans, and he didn't think I cared enough for fish to pay $350.00 for one! What kind of fish would be worth $350.00 anyway?

Somewhere amidst all this, I ambled into the family room and got the story. LaVerne hadn't been paid for a service

37

rendered, and it was rectified immediately. Suddenly, we were $350.00 richer than we had been when we had gotten out of bed that morning!

I still had one more fish to land because part of that money belonged to God, and social security needed to be taken out—plus the fact that we were still short. So I went a-fishing! The tax deadline, February seventeenth, came. I checked the mail. There wasn't any fish! Did you ever shed great big hot tears and feel that God had failed you? Or more to the point, that somehow you had failed Him and not measured up to the answer to your prayers? Now God didn't say in His Word, "Lois Morse gets two big fat fish by February seventeenth!" He did say He would take care of our needs, and we were plainly in need.

The next morning He jarred my whole being with the thought, "You felt you trusted Me too much—but really, you didn't trust Me enough! Because you trusted Me up to the deadline but not through the deadline, up to the trouble but not through the trouble, up to the end of your spoken prayers but not through your prayers yet unspoken."

So I got that fishing pole back in my hands and said, "The deadline is over! I trust to the deadline, through the deadline, around the deadline, over the deadline, under the deadline!"

I thought about Abraham. Twice God took him through his "deadlines," and he trusted Him through each one. When God told him He'd give him a son, He waited till Sarah was "too old" to bear a child and until Abraham's body was as good as dead.[2] Then He said, "O.K., now that your deadline is over, My time has come!" Isaac was born. Another time God led Abraham and Isaac up to a mountain. Abraham built an altar there, bound his son, and laid him on it. He stretched out his hand and took the knife to slay him.[3] When Abraham's deadline was over, God's deadline came! It was not when Isaac was laid on the altar, but when Abraham raised the knife! God saved Isaac and made Abraham great.

We sometimes get depressed because our vision is finite, and we just can't see things from God's point of view.

Can't you see Daniel being lowered into the lion's den[4] and hear someone saying, "Whoops, Lord, You missed the deadline!" Oh, no, He didn't. God's deadline was not the opening of the lion's den, but the closing of the lions' mouths. God was right on time as He always is!

Can't you see Shadrach, Meshach, and Abednego being thrown into the fiery furnace[5] and hear someone saying, "Oh, oh, Lord, You missed the deadline!" Oh, no, He didn't. God's deadline was not the opening of the door of the furnace, but deliverance in the midst of the fire! God was right on time.

Can't you see Pharaoh's chariots and horsemen pursuing the Israelites as they crossed the Red Sea[6] and hear someone saying, "Look now, Lord, You missed the deadline!" Oh, no, He didn't. God's deadline was not this side of the Red Sea, but the far side! God was right on time.

Can't you see Lazarus on his bed sick unto death, and then dying,[7] and hear someone saying, "It's too bad this time, Lord; You missed the deadline!" Oh, no, He didn't. God's deadline was not this side of the grave, but the other side! God was four days late, but God was right on time.

Now I understand while I'm saying all of this that sometimes God's people aren't delivered in the way we've been talking about. The book of Hebrews makes it pretty plain that even though some through faith "conquered kingdoms, performed acts of righteousness, obtained promises, shut the mouths of lions, quenched the power of fire, escaped the edge of the sword" (Hebrews 11:33, 34, NAS), that still others through faith "experienced mockings and scourgings, yes, also chains and imprisonment. They were stoned, they were sawn in two, they were tempted, they were put to death with the sword" (Hebrews 11:36, 37, NAS). When God doesn't deliver us according to our way of thinking, that's God's business. The important thing for us to remember is that we will not miss any good thing or be deprived of any real need—as God sees it!

I didn't catch my second fish, and that's God's business. The thing I want to say is this: Sometimes we sit on the shoreline cleaning our fishing gear with our tears, assuming our treasured dreams are really not for us just because we've passed our deadline. Do you know what? We might miss out on the most special blessing God has in mind for us because we put our fishing rod down too soon! If God does give us that big fish—if that's part of His will for our lives—we're not going to be saying, "Hey, look what my prayers did! Look what my faith did! It's Show-and-Tell time!" We're going to be falling down on our knees and saying the same thing Peter said after he got his big catch, "Go away from me, Lord; I am a sinful man!" (Luke 5:8, New International Version).

We really do need to hold each other's arms up while we're holding our fishing rods because sometimes we sit there for such a long time, and we get tired and discouraged. At least, I know I do! But God is the one who puts the fish in the water! He knows just how many fish we need, and when we need each one.

We really do need God!

---

[1]Matthew 17:24-27.
[2]Hebrews 11:11-12.
[3]Genesis 22:1-14.
[4]Daniel 6.
[5]Daniel 3.
[6]Exodus 14.
[7]John 11:1-46.

Make Friends With

God's World

I love you, people of the world!

Your triumphs and failings, written in bold headlines for all the world to see, spell out many of the triumphs and failings of those of us who call ourselves Christian.

You fashion for yourselves gods made of wood and stone. We fashion for ourselves gods of our own imaginings and fail to see them because their form is less definitive.

You take the name of the Lord in vain and utter vile profanity and swearing in the streets. We turn our curses inward and suffer from all sorts of maladies and diseases.

You buy and sell on Sundays and keep no day holy unto the Lord. We worship the Lord on Sunday mornings and evenings and sell Him for our own interests in the afternoons.

You openly and brazenly inflict harm upon your parents who bore you. We smite our parents through indifference.

You take up the sword and brutally murder your neighbor. We wield the homemade weapons of hatred and envy and kill in a more socially acceptable fashion.

You commit adultery, luring others in the streets and causing open shame. We retire to our own private chambers and lust in the secrecy of our hearts.

You steal by taking. We steal by withholding.

You stand in the courtrooms of the land and bear false witness against your neighbor. We bear false witness against ourselves by wearing a mask and posing as something we are not.

41

You covet that which is your neighbor's and cause wars to get it. We covet that which is our neighbor's and forget him in order to forget what he has.

We are all sinners—acting our different stages of rebellion and acceptance, deterioration and growth.

Then wherein lies the difference between us?

You try to pull yourselves up by your own bootstraps. We take off our shoes and kneel at the foot of the cross beneath the naked, pierced feet of the Son of God—who loved us all and gave himself for us all that, through Him, we might find redemption from sin, strength for the day, and the hope of everlasting life.

Part Two

Enlarge Your Heart

Open Your Heart

Dorothy discovered something shining in a ray of sunshine that fell between the trees. She ran to the place, and then stopped short with a cry of surprise.

One of the big trees had been partly chopped through, and standing beside it, with an uplifted axe in his hands, was a man made entirely of tin. His head and arms and legs were jointed upon his body, but he stood perfectly motionless, as if he could not stir at all.

Dorothy looked at him in amazement, and so did the Scarecrow, while Toto barked sharply and made a snap at the tin legs, which hurt his teeth.

"Did you groan?" asked Dorothy.

"Yes," answered the tin man, "I did. I've been groaning for more than a year, and no one has ever heard me before or come to help me."

"What can I do for you?" she inquired softly, for she was moved by the sad voice in which the man spoke.

"Get an oil can and oil my joints," he answered. "They are rusted so badly that I cannot move them at all; if I am well oiled I shall soon be all right again.... How did you happen to be here?"

"We are on our way to the Emerald City, to see the great Oz," she answered, "and we stopped at your cottage to pass the night."

"Why do you wish to see Oz?" he asked.

"I want him to send me back to Kansas, and the Scarecrow wants him to put a few brains into his head," she replied.

The Tin Woodman appeared to think deeply for a moment. Then he said:

"Do you suppose Oz could give me a heart?"

"Why, I guess so," Dorothy answered. "It would be as easy as to give the Scarecrow brains."

"True," the Tin Woodman returned. "So, if you will allow me to join your party, I will also go to the Emerald City and ask Oz to help."

"Come along," said the Scarecrow heartily; and Dorothy added that she would be pleased to have his company. So the Tin Woodman shouldered his ax and they all passed through the forest until they came to the road that was paved with yellow brick.

As they traveled, the Tin Woodman told Dorothy and the Scarecrow his story. Finally he said, "While I was in love I was the happiest man on earth; but no one can love who has not a heart, and so I am resolved to ask Oz to give me one. If he does, I will go back to the Munchkin maiden and marry her."

Both Dorothy and the Scarecrow had been greatly interested in the story of the Tin woodman, and now they knew why he was so anxious to get a new heart.

"All the same," said the Scarecrow, "I shall ask for brains instead of a heart; for a fool would not know what to do with a heart if he had one."

"I shall take the heart," returned the Tin Woodman; for brains do not make one happy, and happiness is the best thing in the world."

* * * * *

We all know what it means to lose our hearts. We've lost them over people. We've lost them over circumstances. We've lost them over things. In the losing, we've felt we never would find real happiness again. Sometimes we've lost them over some joy not yet tasted.

I remember sitting one afternoon in an auditorium filled with women. A dear sister in Christ who was about ninety years of age was standing beside the pulpit reciting poetry from memory. She closed her recitation with a piece of writing which had been given to her by a professional entertainer:

My Wild White Rose

It was peeping through the brambles, that little wild white rose,
Where the hawthorne hedge was planted, my garden to enclose.
All beyond was fern and heather, on the breezy open moor,
All within was sun and shelter and a wealth of beauty's store.
But I did not heed the fragrance of the flowerlet or the tree,
For my eyes were on that rosebud, and it grew too high for me.

In vain I strove to reach it, through its tangled mass of green,
It only bowed and nodded behind its thorny screen.
Yet through that summer morning, I lingered near the spot,

O why do things seem sweeter, if we possess them not?
My garden buds were blooming, but all that I could see,
Was that little mocking white rose, hanging just too high for me.

So in life's wider garden, there are buds of promise too,
Beyond our reach to gather, but not beyond our view.
And like the little charmer that tempted me astray,
They steal out half the brightness of many a summer day.
O hearts that fail with longing, for some forbidden tree,
Look up! and learn a lesson, from my white rose and me.

'twere wiser far to number the blessings at my feet,
Than ever to be sighing for just one bud more sweet.
My sunshine and my shadows fall from a Pierced Hand,
I can surely trust His wisdom, since His heart I understand,
And maybe, in the morning, when His blessed face I see,
He will tell me why my white rose was just too high for me.

—Author Unknown

When we yearn inordinately for some blessing God has
not given, whatever our "little wild white rose" might be, we
make an idol out of it. Idols are heavy and burdensome
because they have to be carried around, whereas it was always God's intention to carry His worshipers. Isaiah pictures
for us the contrast:

Bel has bowed down, Nebo stoops over;[1]
Their images are consigned to the beasts and the
    cattle.
The things that you carry are burdensome,
A load for the weary beast.
They stooped over, they have bowed down together;
They could not rescue the burden,
But have themselves gone into captivity.

"Listen to Me, O house of Jacob,
And all the remnant of the house of Israel,
You who have been borne by Me from birth,
And have been carried from the womb;
Even to your old age, I shall be the same,
And even to your graying years I shall bear you!
I have done it, and I shall carry you;
And I shall bear you, and I shall deliver you."

(Isaiah 46:1-4, NAS)

47

Every single morning that you and I awaken on this earth, we have two choices stretched out before us. Either we can carry our idols—the people, the circumstances, the things for which we yearn and which weigh us down till we have no heart to go on—or we can open our hearts and ask God to carry us wherever He wills.

Sometimes, because we are just learning to walk by faith, it's scary to let go and let God carry us, because we know He'll take us where *He* wants to go, not necessarily where *we* want to go. We get frightened about being in His arms and scramble down so that our own two legs can take us in the direction of "life's best." Sometimes it's so much easier to obey certain commands than it is to trust. So instead of losing heart because of life's situations and feeling we've lost all hope for happiness, God wants us to trust Him to help us gain heart in dealing with all our difficult circumstances. It takes us so long to understand that God loves us far more than we love ourselves, that He understands us far more than we understand ourselves, and that His way is best.

Earlier in my book, I mentioned and defined a problem which many women suffer called anorexia nervosa, "a refusal to eat that can lead to extreme loss of weight, hormonal disturbances, and even death ..."[2] I have discovered other forms of this disorder among women which I have chosen to call spiritual anorexia nervosa and emotional anorexia nervosa. I made reference to spiritual anorexia nervosa in a previous chapter. Now, I would like to have you consider with me the disorder, emotional anorexia nervosa, which causes women to lose heart.

Emotional anorexia nervosa begins when a woman stands aloof from people in general, or a person in particular, and says, on a conscious or unconscious level, "I don't need you." Somewhere in her development someone on whom she needed to lean let her down, and she enters womanhood with an inability to trust.

A woman who is suffering from emotional anorexia nervosa is unable, psychologically, to receive nourishment from others unless she dictates the relationship and remains in control. She is capable of leaning very heavily on another person until something happens which does not meet with her pleasure or approval. At that point in time she assumes a stiff posture and says in self-defense, "I don't need you." To her way of thinking, remaining in control and not needing the person who has let her down will save her from ever again receiving a hurt she cannot handle.

The pain of emotional anorexia nervosa is especially severe in a woman who is married, because needing her husband and being able to give herself into his keeping is foundational to her enjoying her marriage. Unfortunately, this is precisely what she cannot do.

Sadly, emotional anorexia nervosa is like a cancer which spreads from the kitchen to the living room, to the family room, to the bedroom until literally, every area of her life is affected. Her emotional joints become so rusty that she is not able to function normally. With the Tin Woodman, she stands in place and waits for help to come.

She reaches the place where she is unable, psychologically, to reach out for help, and even though she is starving emotionally, she may groan for a long time before help arrives. She finds herself in much the same position as the Tin Woodman who said, "I've been groaning for more than a year, and no one has ever heard me before or come to help me."

A woman suffering from emotional anorexia nervosa usually has an ax to grind over her misfortune, which is *very real,* and is unable, psychologically, to lay it down. Her posture is much the same as that of the Tin Woodman who stood with an uplifted ax in his hands.

Countless women suffer from emotional anorexia nervosa to varying degrees of intensity. The beginning of healing comes when a woman's cries for help are heard, and the oil of human kindness is received in sufficient amounts over a sufficient period of time to enable her to bend her rusty emotional joints. All who receive healing can easily identify with the Tin Woodman's sigh of satisfaction as he lowered his ax and leaned it against the tree. "This is a great comfort," he said. "I have been holding that ax in the air ever since I rusted, and I'm glad to be able to put it down at last."

To every woman suffering from emotional anorexia nervosa, God stretches out His arms of love and cries:

"Come to Me, all who are weary and heavy laden
and I will give you rest. Take My yoke upon you,

and learn from Me, for I am gentle and humble in
heart; and you shall find rest for your souls.
For My yoke is easy, and My load is light."
                                    (Matthew 11:28-30, NAS)

There's a Tin Woodman inside of you who is traveling with you on the road that leads to the city of God. Make friends with your heart. Take it by the hand and help it to carry all of its idols to your heavenly Father and to leave its dearest dreams in His keeping. Open your heart to Him for He is a Specialist at fixing broken hearts and wings and things.

The Little Angel With the Broken Wing

The little angel was tired of walking. If only her wing hadn't gotten broken, she could have completed her mission on earth and been back in Heaven by now. Instead, here she was, stumbling along a busy thoroughfare on earth looking for someone to fix her broken wing. Since she was invisible to human eyes, folks just passed her by—intent on their own errands.

She didn't know how to make contact with people, but she prayed a lot. She knew God cared about what had happened to her. In fact, right after her accident (her wing had gotten caught on the branch of a tree on the way down) she was convinced He would send a chariot from Heaven to fetch her. God had explained to the little angel that since she was on earth He would need to use some other means of helping her. But how? she wondered. She certainly couldn't fix her own wing, and how could anyone else help her when she couldn't even be seen?

She studied the matter for a long time. One day she devised a plan. Because she was an angel, she had the power to lose herself in someone else. So she began looking around for someone whose life she could share.

One day she saw a beautiful girl whose body was just perfect. "I'll become part of her," she cried, "and then my broken wing will be healed through her strength!" So she became part of the beautiful girl, but her wing didn't change.

In time, the little angel began to feel very uncomfortable about the whole arrangement. The girl didn't need healing and therefore didn't come into contact with anyone who might have healed the little angel who lived inside her.

So she left the beautiful girl and began looking around again. This time she knew she needed to find someone who was not yet whole—hoping that person would seek healing so she, too, could be healed.

In time, she saw another little girl who was limping. "This is perfect for me!" she cried. So she became part of the crippled girl. The crippled girl, though she longed to be whole, didn't know where to go for healing. So the little angel was no better off than before. So she left her.

Then one day she got an idea. Why not ask for help? So she got a pen and made a big sign: "HELP WANTED. An angel with a broken wing cannot return to Heaven. Needs healing. Anyone who knows how to fix a broken wing please write directions on this sheet of paper."

She sat down beside the sign to see what would happen. Lots of people read the sign. Most just shook their heads, not knowing what to make of it, and went on about their business.

Then one day a young lad walked by and stopped to read the sign. He sighed a big sigh. "The little angel forgot to leave her address," he said. "How can anyone help her?" And he walked away.

The little angel hadn't thought of that problem and wondered what to do. Then she added a P. S. to her sign: "It doesn't matter where I live. I will return and read what you write for me."

Once again she sat down by her sign and waited. Again folks passed by. They stayed a little longer to read the P.S. but moved on as usual.

She decided to tear up her sign and write another. She wrote it this way: "An angel has come down from Heaven and cannot return. Therefore, she will use her time on earth to tell you everything she has seen in Heaven and everything she knows about God. Heaven is a real place to her, and God is real." Then she wrote a beautiful description of Heaven as she remembered it and a beautiful description of God. Folks stopped to read the sign. They began sitting down around it, and talking together about the things that had been written. They wondered if the words of the little angel were true.

When God looked down and saw that the little angel had sought to draw men's attention to Him instead of being

51

altogether preoccupied with her broken wing, He was pleased. He sent an angel from Heaven to minister to her special needs. As she felt healing taking place within her, she praised God, thanked Him profusely, and became so excited she began to fly. Her wings propelled her into space. She flew back to Heaven and once again took up her heavenly chores.

People continued to stop by her sign. They continued to talk about Heaven, God, and the little angel. But they never knew it was only because of her broken wing they had been given a glimpse of Heaven and of God as she remembered them.

The Size and Shape of Happiness

To say, "If you actively pursue happiness, it will elude you," makes about as much sense as telling a farmer, "If you actively pursue a crop of potatoes, you'll end up with cucumbers instead." Both crops come to the one who does things God's way with an eye to the harvest, be it potatoes or joy.

In an age when men are traveling into space to search for the unknown, I decided to take a journey into life to search for something almost as mysterious as the moon and Mars—*my own personal happiness!*

As I walked along life's pathway, intent on my search, I saw an old man resting by the side of the road. Mistaking his age for wisdom, I approached him and said, "Sir, can you tell me the size and shape of happiness? For I have ventured far from my home to find it."

He lifted his weather-beaten face to mine and cradled my question in his thoughts. Then he spoke, "Listen carefully, my friend, and I will tell you what happiness is. Once I was young, and all of life was before me. Now I am old and at the end of everything for which I have lived. To be happy is to be young again!"

I thanked him heartily for his answer and hastened on down the road, feeling self-confident in my search. Shortly, I noticed a young man walking toward me. I trembled with excitement and ran to meet him. I thought that truly I had come to the end of my search! As I drew nearer, I saw that though he was young, there was a deep sadness in his eyes. I was inwardly thrown by this. But I emboldened myself because of my search and addressed him saying, "My young sir, I have ventured far from my home in my quest for happiness. In the course of my travels, I met an old man who told me that happiness is youth. Therefore, Sir, when I saw you, I thought that surely happiness would be yours."

He stared at me in disbelief and said, "My friend, think not that happiness is youth. For I have youth. But I have lost the wife of my youth, my beloved. We were betrothed but a year and a day when I laid her away in the earth. Now I walk alone."

When I saw the deep agony of his soul, I turned from questioning him and continued on my way. As I journeyed, I thought: Happiness is not youth, but having a mate.

I happened upon a man and a woman walking hand in hand down the road together. I breathed a sigh of relief, thinking that at last I had discovered happiness. I approached them with courage in my heart and said, "My good friends, can you tell me the size and shape of happiness? For I have ventured far from my home to find it. In my travels I met an old man who told me that happiness is youth, but when I found a young lad, he denied it. He told me that happiness is having a mate. When I saw the two of you traveling side by side together, I thought: Surely happiness is here.

When I had finished speaking, their faces left mine and embraced each other with longing. Tears filled their eyes as they said, "Lo, these many years we have yearned for a child. Now the time for bearing children is over. How, then, do you think that happiness is ours?"

As I parted from them, I carried within my soul their sorrow. For I could see that happiness was not to be had simply because a man and a woman walked side by side together.

As I journeyed on, I saw a husband and his wife walking down the road with their child beside them. I ran quickly to their side, hoping—almost fearing to hope—that at last I had found happiness. I greeted them and said, "My friends, I have seen you walking together with your child. Surely, as I look upon her face, I can see that she bears your very image. Can you tell me the size and shape of happiness? I have ventured far from my home to find it. But when I make inquiry, one person tells me one thing and another another, so that I do not know any longer who or what to believe. Tell me, have you found happiness?"

As the father faced me, I saw lines of weariness etched deeply in his face, and the mother's eyes reflected nothing but bitterness and sorrow. They spoke to me with scornful voices and said, "Lo, this our child has gone astray and has given us nothing but shame. How then can you think that happiness is ours?" I walked away from them. My heart was exceedingly heavy within me. For I wanted desperately to discover the size and shape of happiness.

As I thought on these things, I met a man whom many considered to be wise. I hastened to him and plunged into my story without even so much as giving him a chance to speak, for my mind was deeply troubled. When I had finished speaking, he opened his mouth and said, "My daughter, you err in thinking that happiness comes in one certain size and shape. For no matter how richly blessed a woman may be, she always carries on her shoulder an empty bag. This empty bag represents something in her life that is missing. She interprets this missing thing as happiness, and as happiness is gathered, each bag assumes a different size and shape. For truly each woman carries her own unique set of burdens and desires.

"And herein is the problem compounded, my daughter. Every woman believes that happiness consists of that thing which is missing in her own life. If her neighbor possesses something which is the same size and shape of that which she covets, she thinks that her neighbor has found happiness. She fails to see the empty bag thrown across her neighbor's shoulder. So each woman eyes her neighbor with envy instead of understanding, and wisdom is altogether lost."

Happiness is not just filling an empty bag, although there is indeed happiness when one's empty bag is filled.

Happiness is needing to be loved and believing that Jesus loves you and will supply the human love that you need.

Happiness is having real needs and believing that God "shall supply all your needs according to His riches in glory in Christ Jesus" (Philippians 4:19, NAS).

Happiness is having special longings and being able to leave them in God's hands believing that He "is able to do exceeding abundantly beyond all that we ask or think, according to the power that works within us" (Ephesians 3:20, NAS).

Happiness is having sorrows and believing that God "causes all things to work together for good to those who love God, to those who are called according to His purpose" (Romans 8:28, NAS).

Happiness is living the questions and believing that God is the answer.

---

[1]"Bel and Nebo were the supreme deities of the Babylonians, Bel being Baal in Hebrew and meaning 'Lord'; Nebo was the god of learning, whose chief seat of worship was in Borsippa near Babylon. Idols had to be carried by worshipers. God carries His worshipers from time of birth." Footnote on Isaiah 46:1,3, (New Berkeley Version).

[2]Jeffrey R. M. Knuz, MD, Editor-in-Chief, *The American Medial Association Family Medical Guide* (New York: Random House, Inc., 1982), p. 710.

No Greater Joy

The sun arose as a bridegroom coming out of his chamber
    and thought no joy greater than his
    as he opened the sleepy eyelids of men
    and bade them start their labors for the day.
The moon stood high above the earth
    and thought no joy greater than hers
    as she stirred the sleeping passions of men
    and awakened in them their deepest dreams.
The morning stars sang together in the heavens
    and thought no joy greater than theirs
    as they lit up the galaxies of space
    and led men on their courses.
The waves of the sea tossed against the sandy shores
    and thought no joy greater than theirs
    as they danced to the drumbeat of the moon and the winds
    and carried in their bosom boys and girls at play.
The flowers of the fields swayed to the rhythm of the winds
    and thought no joy greater than theirs
    as they skipped in time with the universe
    and perfumed the dwelling places of men.
But all of these stopped short in their rejoicing
and held their breath as they bowed to the joy of another—
    a child of God led by the hand of God
    walking straight into the sunlight of His dreams!

Gain Heart by

Conquering Unhappiness

A French philosopher once said, "The whole world is on a mad quest for security and happiness."[1] Now I have no idea what was in the mind of this philosopher when he penned those lines, but the more I thought about them the more they intrigued me. Why "the whole world"?

Why isn't it just one or two persons who are on this mad quest for happiness—or a hundred or a thousand? Why isn't it just the Germans or the French or the English? Why isn't it just those who live north of the equator or those who live south of the equator? Why isn't it just Easterners or Westerners? Why isn't it just people who live in the big cities of the world or people who live in small towns and villages? Why "the whole world"?

Well, for the same reason that fish swim and birds fly. Because God made them that way. Why is the whole world on a mad quest for happiness? Because when God created man and woman, He put within them the instinct for happiness. This instinct inside of man is as real and as powerful as the homing instinct inside of Lassie. You may remember that tattered, tricolored collie bounding one thousand dogged miles to lick brokenhearted Roddy McDowall's cheek in the classic film of 1943.

Speaking of the homing instinct, my father once shared with me an article he had saved from *The Enquirer Magazine* entitled, "How *Does* Lassie Get Home?" Beneath the caption were these words: "In the forty years since that wonderful collie crossed hundreds of miles of movie screen, man has discovered lasers, penicillin and moon rockets—but not the secret of the *HOMING SENSE.*"

How does a dog or cat pick the right direction to head and avoid going astray? "What's particularly baffling," continues the writer, Gordon Lee Burgett, "is how the pets find masters who have moved to areas where the creatures have never been."[2] We experienced this once with a cat of ours who left home before we moved to the opposite side of the city, and he just appeared one day in our back yard several years later to the delight of all of us.

God put that homing instinct inside of Lassie when He created him, and God put the instinct for happiness inside each one of us when He created us. I believe, like the homing instinct, it was intended to help us find our way Home and to keep us from stopping two blocks from happiness.

Newell Dwight Hillis, author of the book, *The Quest of Happiness,* notes "This instinct for happiness is as deeply embedded in man's nature as the instinct of life itself."[3] It's not something evil! It's not something to be ignored or shoved aside while we get on with the "important things of life"! It *is* an important part of life *if it is God-directed.* How I love those lines written by Irenaeus in the second century, "The Glory of God is a human being who is fully alive!"[4]

Jesus didn't say, "I am come that you might cope." He said, "I came that they might have life, and might have it abundantly" (John 10:10, NAS).

I think of Hannah Whitall Smith's comments in her book, *The God of All Comfort:* "If I were a poor sheep, wandering in the wilderness, and I were to see some poor, wretched, sick-looking sheep peeping out of a fold, and calling me to come in, and I were to look into the fold, and should see it hard, bare, and uncomfortable, I do not think I would be much tempted to go into such a fold."[5]

There will be sorrow in our lives. Christ himself was a "man of sorrows, and acquainted with grief" (Isaiah 53:3, NAS), but Christ was not a man of unhappiness. Godly sorrow is pure grief. It is always filled with the presence of God himself. Unhappiness is an alloy—an emotional substance mixing sorrow together with one or more negative, sinful emotions such as bitterness, unforgiveness, anger, etc.

Whether we are experiencing sorrow or joy, God wants us to be happy. He put the instinct for happiness inside of us to goad us on until we each work out the mystery of our own personal happiness.

For half a century now I have been reaching out for happiness. At the same time, God has been reaching out to me.

He loved me so much and wanted so badly for me to be happy that He kept trying in every possible way to get through to me—no matter how blind I was, or no matter how stubborn. It just never dawned on me that He was really all that concerned about my personal happiness. I knew He wanted me to be good, and I tried to be good. I knew He wanted me to serve Him, and I went halfway around the world to do that! But my happiness? Well, that was another matter. There had been too many tears, too much struggling, too many trials, and too much suffering.

One morning tears came to my eyes as I meditated on a Bible passage that spoke to me so deeply because it reflected my faulty feelings about God. Do you remember when Joseph's brothers returned to him for the second time to buy grain during the severe famine? They brought with them Benjamin, Joseph's youngest brother, and double payment for the money they had found in their sacks. When they arrived, they were brought to Joseph's house. The Bible says, "But being taken into Joseph's house made them afraid, suspecting, 'We are being brought in because of the money that was returned to our sacks on the first trip; he will accuse us, overpower us, make us his slaves and appropriate our donkeys'" (Genesis 43:18, Berkeley Version of the Bible).

Oh, the times that I have been summoned into God's presence! I thought, as did Joseph's brothers, "He's called me here to accuse me, to overpower me, to make me His slave, and even to appropriate my precious donkeys." I didn't understand the heart of the Father as illustrated a few verses later in Joseph's own motives for calling his brothers to his house. "Then Joseph hurried away, for he was deeply moved over his brother; so he stepped into a room and wept. Then he washed his face, came out and mastered his emotions. He said, 'Serve dinner!'" (Genesis 43:30, 31, Berkeley Version of the Bible).

I thought of those precious lines in Isaiah, "Israel is my vineyard; I, the Lord, will tend the fruitful vines; every day I'll water them, and day and night I'll watch to keep all enemies

59

away" (Isaiah 27:3, The Living Bible). God was watching over my vineyard. He was my Keeper. He was guarding me day and night. When He saw an enemy coming—when He saw something in my life that was keeping me from enjoying the wonderful dinner he had prepared, or when He saw something in me that was interfering with my personal happiness—He would alter my circumstances, or show me my wrong. At other times, when He didn't see fit to change my circumstances or I wasn't involved in any wrong doing, He would simply say, "Trust me! I'm using this to make something beautiful out of your life." Then He would step back into the main room and say, *"Dinner is served!"*

One of the things God has taught me about happiness is that it is terribly complex. It's not the missing piece of a puzzle—it's the whole puzzle! It's not a single event—it's a maturing process, both emotionally and spiritually.

One day while attending a workshop in psychology, I learned that joy is the last emotion developed inside a child:

From birth to 3 months, a child experiences *distress* and *delight.*

From 3 months to 6 months, he experiences anger and *disgust.*

From 6 months to 12 months, he experiences fear and *elation*

From 12 months to 18 months, he experiences affection for adults and children

From 18 months to 24 months, he experiences *jealousy* and *joy*

Joy is a very complex emotion. Children who are battered or who for some reason are frozen in their emotional development very deeply reflect the absence of joy.

I never will forget sitting in an empty auditorium hours after I had delivered my message there. I say, the auditorium was empty, but there was a young girl sitting beside me who was too withdrawn to freely open her heart. She handed me several pieces of paper on which someone had written part of her life story. I sat there, and this is what I read in part. (I have taken the liberty of changing the names.)

"'God, I'm lonely'—Mary's cry whipped through the darkness with an angry force as though trying desperately to reach into Heaven itself.... It was a cancer that could not be cured. 'Oh God, help me, when will it end? There's no one but You to help me now. God, if just one person would acknowledge that I am alive and that I have feelings. If just one person would reach out to me and care, but they won't. Oh God, I give up!'

"It was this prayer that marked Mary's surrender. Her body relaxed, eyes closed she ceased to fight loneliness and let it penetrate her being. It would fill her up and become her friend. Now it wouldn't hurt her anymore because if she never knew happiness or the comfort of a friend—she'd not know what she was missing. She would become so callous to anything that sought to penetrate the barrier she was forming in her mind, that being lonely no longer mattered. It is just a state of being. Her reasoning was that as long as she had her own inner strength and her mind then what more— who else did she need. By turning her mind inward, she would not be open to the pain other people brought, and then she could survive—but only that, survive....

"When forced to climb into herself, Mary was confronted with a naked and shameless look at who she really was. The memories of her past flooded her being till shaking with sobs she cried out for God again. She could not bear the pain those visions of years past were bringing. Memories of her father coming home drunk to his seven children and a nagging wife. He would beat the kids and laugh insanely as they lay crying on the floor. The alcohol had destroyed him, she knew, but she still could not forgive him for his plots and schemes to rid himself of his children. Leaving them to die in the mountains, he returned three months later surprised to see they had somehow managed to stay alive.

"These memories were mild compared to the one that entered her mind now. This one had brought many nightmares in years past, but she thought she had conquered it. Now it came back as vivid and real as if it were happening again. She could see her father yelling insanely, kicking her four-year-old brother who was screaming and writhing on the floor. Kicking him over and over telling him to shut up. If only he had stopped crying, but he couldn't. He was just a child—a baby. Why couldn't her father have understood that? Then it happened.... before she realized what he was doing, her father had tied the rope around little Michael's neck and strung him from the pipe that ran across the ceiling of their shabby apartment. There was a scream . . . a snap . . . and then, suddenly, the room was still. Only the sound of the creaking rope could be heard as she, her mother, and her father gazed at Michael's body. Mary screamed and then the world went black as her father knocked her to the ground.

"Mary never told anyone, not even her sisters and brothers about what she had seen. She had locked it up in her mind, but somehow it escaped at night and haunted her in her dreams.

"Two days after the hanging, Mary left home. She could not bear to even look at the disgusting figure of a man who would kill his own son. She had dressed in the only rags she owned and walked silent and alone down the dark streets of the ghetto. . . ."

"Time goes on, life goes on," Mary said. "For some it's only just begun. For others no time is left at all. For me?—I do not know. Time froze when he left . . . pain says I am still alive—but will I ever live again?"

We all have real needs that need to be met in order to even have the capacity to be happy emotionally—including experiencing the love of a mother and a father. To walk past some individuals and say flippantly, "Be happy," would be about as pointless as walking past a baby's crib and saying to the infant, "Rise up and walk," or as cruel as walking up to a cancer patient and saying, "Be well." *Some things are beyond our grasp save for the ministration of others:*

> He stood behind the pulpit, Lord,
> and spoke for a long time
> about Your divinity.
> The woman didn't mean to be disrespectful,
> but her head began to nod
> while her eyes closed in drowsiness.
> Through the cloudiness
> her mind was accepting the fact
> that You were divine,
> But it was her heart that hurt,
> not her head!
> And somehow, he wasn't reaching that.
> Then one day someone told her
> that You loved her with the love
> of both a mother and a father.

And two people wrapped their arms
around her and held her close.
As she snuggled on their shoulders,
she closed her eyes in perfect peace
and dreamed of Your divinity
and how wonderful it must be!

Several months after being with Mary I received a letter from her. I share the closing paragraph with you.

"My life is being completely changed around. I thank God for many years of prayers that were answered in a matter of weeks. I've waited so long to be happy and to feel that I belonged in a family that loves me for who I am, and not pretending to love me for what I can give them or do for them. Finally, I've found someone who is concerned for my well-being and who takes care of me when I'm sick, and who sits by my side when I'm sad or lonely, and who is not afraid to say to me, 'I love you' and really mean it. Never have I felt so comfortable and secure about my future now that the emptiness inside is slowly being filled one day at a time. It's a dream come true! And I owe it all to God!"

I think back on that day when I held this young girl in my arms, talked with her, and prayed with her in that empty auditorium, and I smile when I recall a sentence I heard on the radio one day "For God so loved the world He didn't send a committee!"

So often it's one special person that we need, and God cares. He cares about every single need of every single child of His whether that need is a person, some material blessing, some circumstance, or the need for character building. Whatever it may be, if it's a real need as God sees it, "My God shall supply all your needs according to His riches in glory in Christ Jesus" (Philippians 4:19, NAS). If not through one person, then through another. God has a marvelous backup system to fill up those deep cracks and crevices where people have failed us, and where we, in turn, have failed others.

Happiness is not only a maturing process emotionally. It is also a maturing process spiritually. Like the homing instinct which leads to the bonding that takes place between a pet and his master, the instinct for happiness ushers in the bonding that takes place between God and His spiritual offspring.

The newspaper article I quoted regarding Lassie and the homing instinct makes this observation:

"Konrad Lorenz, the Nobel Prize-winning ethologist, relates homing to the critical 'bonding' that takes place when a pet and master are exposed to each other during key periods of the pet's development. During that time, the pet becomes attached to its master as it would normally to others of its own species. Its keeper becomes its social focus. Simultaneously, it becomes attached to its physical surroundings.

"Where it lives becomes its home range, and its 'homing instinct' is to return to the place, or person, to which it became bonded. Since bonding takes place over a period of time in a young animal's life, kittens or puppies not yet fully bonded will often willingly swap masters simply for a meal. But older pets, particularly a mother separated from her offspring, will travel great distances to get 'home.'"[6]

This bonding process, designed by God into His creation, is fascinating. It takes place between a mother, father, and child during the emotional development of the child, until somewhere around the age of two the child is capable of experiencing joy. It also takes place between God and each of His children.

Sometimes during this bonding process, Christians who are not yet fully bonded to their Master may, like kittens and puppies, willingly swap masters, simply for a meal. This is called *sin.* Hopefully, in due process of time, we will become so attached to our Master and will so love every word that proceeds out of His mouth that swapping Him for anyone or anything in all of this world will never even enter our minds. When this time comes, we are going to begin to experience what a child normally experiences at the age of two—**JOY!**

I believe there are two sides to happiness—God's side and our side. I believe that God's side, in a nutshell, is wrapped up in the promise already quoted, "And my God shall supply all your needs according to His riches in glory in Christ Jesus" (Philippians 4:19, NAS). I believe that our side, in a nutshell, is wrapped up in the words of the chorus, "Trust and obey, for there's no other way to be happy in Jesus, but to trust and obey."

Real, genuine happiness doesn't come easily. We don't learn to trust and obey overnight. Neither does God supply all of our needs in a twenty-four-hour period of time. We experience different needs during different phases of our growth, and God supplies those needs in accordance with His wisdom and timetable.

Happiness is a bonding process that takes place over a long period of time between God and His children. It's like a plant that grows in your garden. It's a plant when it's only one inch tall, but hopefully it will continue to grow until it reaches its full potential. Even so we should be as happy as we can be—even when we are only one inch tall emotionally and spiritually. It is our blessed privilege and our moral responsibility to grow taller and taller toward fullness of joy until some day—literally and figuratively—we reach the sky. With Newell Dwight Hillis I concur, "The duty of self-denial is not more imperative than the duty of delight."[7]

> "Happy are those who mourn;
> God will comfort them!
> "Happy are the meek;
> they will receive what God has promised!
> "Happy are those whose greatest desire is to do
> what God requires;
> God will satisfy them fully!
> "Happy are those who are merciful to others;
> God will be merciful to them! . . ."
> (Matthew 5:4-7, *Good News for Modern Man*)

God knew that sometimes it would be hard for us to put our lives together because, like a jigsaw puzzle, each life has so many individual pieces. So He did for us what we often do when we work a puzzle. He put all the pieces with the straight edges together when He gave us the Beatitudes so we could put together the frame of our picture. Then He gave us hundreds of pieces in His Word and hundreds more in His personal gifts to us, and said, "Now get to work!"

Sometimes when we can't find a missing piece, we panic. We may even walk away from the puzzle and refuse to work on it. But God says, "Be of good courage! If it's a real need as I see it and part of My will for your life, it will be there. My timing will be perfect. In the meantime, get to work on the other pieces."

Sometimes it seems we spend a lot of time waiting for God to act, and we wonder why problems aren't being resolved in our lives. He may sometimes simply be waiting for us to act. We need to pour over our Bibles as we would pour over the pieces of a giant jigsaw puzzle. With every promise and with every command we find and lock into our lives, the happier we'll be. We also need to thank and praise God for every person and circumstance He has designed or allowed in our lives to fill the grand spectrum of our needs. With every person and with every circumstance we lock into place, the happier we'll be.

God has placed a thousand obstacles in the pathway to hell. One of the highest over which men must climb is the instinct for happiness.

---

[1]Billy Graham, *The Secret of Happiness*, (Garden City, New York: Doubleday & Company, Inc., 1955), p. 1.

[2]Gordon Lee Burgett, "How Does Lassie Get Home?", The Enquirer Magazine, Sunday, November 12, 1978, p. 28.

[3]Newell Dwight Hillis, *The Quest of Happiness* (New York: The Macmillan Company, 1902), p. 5.

[4]John Powell, *Fully Human Fully Alive* (Niles, Illinois: Argus Communications, 1976), p. 7.

[5]Hannah Whitall Smith, *The God of All Comfort*, p. 57. Moody Press. Moody Bible Institute of Chicago. Used by permission.

[6]Burgett, *op. cit.,* p. 31.

[7]Hillis, *op. cit.,* p. 7.

Gain Heart by

Building Self-Esteem

*As water is to a flower, so are encouraging words
to one's self-esteem. God gives the seed.
Man tends it.*

"How fair I am," thought the daffodil as she swayed in the open sunlight. "If only all the other flowers of the field were like me!" As she danced in the summer winds to the music of simply being, she sighed, "Why, I must be the most important of all of God's flowers."

While her boasting was being carried by the winds from one flower to another—for this is how flowers converse—a tear slipped off the tiny petal of a violet. For she deeply questioned her beauty.

Each morning as the sun arose, the little violet would strain with all her might to rise tall like the daffodil. But she couldn't raise herself an inch. After many strenuous efforts, tears covered her soft petals. Passers-by mistook those tears for the early morning dew. They didn't understand the language of flowers, so they didn't know what was happening to the little violet.

Then a mysterious thing happened. The tears of the little violet, having now saturated the ground, began to form a small puddle around her. One day she bowed down and looked at her delicate purple petals reflected in her tears. She saw the beauty that God had created in her and sensed that God had purposely made her different! Inwardly, she began to resent the daffodil's superior air. Her feelings toward herself were so strongly rooted in the daffodil's feel-ings toward her that she began to wither.

Day after day she listened as the daffodil talked on and on about how magnificently God had made her and how God was using her to beautify the earth. But the little violet kept looking into her puddle, and she kept thinking that God must have some purpose for her.

One day a little child came dancing amidst the flowers. She stooped and picked the little violet and took her home. The little violet was so happy to be loved and cherished by the little girl. She tried to stay as fresh and beautiful as she could, but she soon went the way of all flowers and began to fade and die.

The little girl took the little violet, pressed her tenderly in her favorite book, and kept her forever.

* * * * *

J. Chapman Bradley wrote one of the most intriguing stories I have ever read. It's about the little angel who refused to sing the night that Christ was born.[1]

The last rehearsal of the Heavenly choir was almost over. The concert was polished to perfection. Earth would soon receive her Savior King. All was ready—except for one thing!

It so happened that the smallest angel in the heavenly choir was also the problem child of Heaven! His love of mis-chief had thrown things into an uproar on many occasions, and his frankness and independence of thought were a source of embarrassment to the saints.

Gabriel tapped on his trumpet for order. He was about to call for a repetition of the great "Amen" when the little angel suddenly announced, "I'm sorry, Master Gabriel, but I can-not sing."

"Cannot sing?" echoed Gabriel. "Nonsense!"

"No, Master Gabriel," the little angel protested. "I simply cannot sing in the concert tomorrow night. In fact, I posi-tively refuse to sing!"

Gabriel put down his trumpet and stared. A gasp went up from the alabaster rehearsal room. The little angel contin-ued, "You see, I've been doing a lot of thinking about this concert, and I must say I have conscientious objections to participating in it."

"You have conscientious objections!" cried Gabriel. "Is this one of your jokes?"

"No, Sir," replied the little angel gravely. "I am not just joking. As a matter of fact, I must confess I have never been more serious. What I am objecting to is the sentiment of the song we are supposed to sing tomorrow night. 'Peace on earth, good will toward men!' The trouble with a lot of you saints is you simply do not keep up with things. Look down there at that planet earth. Just look at the mess it's in! Peace? All of you angels are singing, 'peace, peace,' when there is no peace. There never was, and there never will be!"

"This is all very interesting," replied Gabriel, "but I'm afraid it's a little late to be thinking about these matters. Even now Mary and Joseph are traveling up the hills on their way to Bethlehem." Gabriel looked at the little angel with obvious annoyance and delivered an ultimatum, "Either you sing with us, or we will excuse you!"

The little angel sighed a deep sigh. Then he raised his hands in a gesture of despair as though to say, "It's useless to try to explain how I feel about that song." Sadly, he left the rehearsal room. Heaven had experienced its first walkout.

God has written the greatest hymnal ever to be published in all the world for all of time. It's called the *Bible,* the Word of God. Inside this grand old Book there are hundreds of songs God wants us to sing. With utmost thoughtfulness and care He has recorded the music and the words.

Here's one: "I will give thanks to Thee, for I am fearfully and wonderfully made" (Psalms 139:14, NAS). We study the words, and then we stand in front of a mirror and carefully scrutinize the image reflected there to see if the sentiment of the song is correct. Being the conscientious people we are, we would hardly want to be caught singing a lie!

As we look in that mirror, we see a nose that's too large and all out of proportion to our facial features, a bustline that's humiliatingly small so that we look and feel more like a developing adolescent than a woman, or hips that are so broad we can never hope to have a streamlined figure no matter how much dieting or exercising we do—or we're too tall or too short. Then we go back to take another look at those words, and we hang our heads sorrowfully and say, "I can't sing that song!" Later, when feelings of actual bitterness well up inside us because of the way God has made us, we cry out, "I positively refuse to sing!" We get up from our seats in the rehearsal room and walk out on God.

Another day when we are looking through our "hymnal," we pause to read the words of still another song: "I am the vine, you are the branches; he who abides in Me, and I in him, he bears much fruit" (John 15:5, NAS). We feel disgruntled inside because God hasn't given us the same gifts we see in some of His other children who are running around doing great things for Him. We sit there and stare at the words of the song just to be sure we're reading them correctly. We say, "I can't sing that song! I positively refuse to sing!"

Then a friend, knowing we are having a problem with self-esteem, comes our way and opens her "hymnbook" to 1 Corinthians 12 and tries to explain to us that we are unique and that God has given to each one of us different gifts according to His will for the uplifting of the whole body of Christ. But we're so low because we don't have the particular gifts we covet. We simply raise our hands in a gesture of despair and say, "What's the use trying to explain how I feel!" We walk out of the rehearsal room and let the other saints do the singing!

Still another day we go to church, and the minister, standing in the pulpit says to the congregation, "Will you please turn with me in your 'hymnal' to Romans 8?" While the organist plays the prelude, we study the words: "There is therefore now no condemnation for those who are in Christ Jesus" (Romans 8:1, NAS). Then we remember that night so long ago when we were morally impure. We look at the words again, and they're all blurred because of our tears. We hang our heads and say, "I can't sing that song!" Others around us are singing and seeming to enjoy themselves, and we quickly dry the tears from our eyes so no one will notice what's going on inside of us. Then we close our "hymnbooks" in a spirit of bitterness and say, "I positively refuse to sing!" Once again we walk out on God.

What is self-esteem all about? Why do we struggle with it so? Where does it really come from? How can we go about getting it?

I remember a very precious moment when LaVerne was standing by the kitchen sink, and Micah, our grandson, was lying on the floor close by. Between them was a baby walker that was just the right size for Micah to push himself around in. Micah was looking intently at the bottom of the walker. When LaVerne noticed him, he said, "You don't have to invent the wheel, Micah! You can go on to other things!"

As we go through life looking intently at the wheels of our natures to discover some basis for our self-esteem, I can just picture God looking down upon us with so much love and compassion in His heart saying, "You don't have to work out your own self-esteem. I've already done that for you! First, by creating you in My image. And second, by recreating you in My image. I want you to go on to other things!" That's what self-esteem is all about on the ground floor level: *CREATION AND RECREATION.*

A long time before psychology was ever thought up by man, God knew we would stand in dire need of self-esteem. In His Word He labeled us as men label garments. The labels God gave to us read something like this: 1) *Exclusive—Fashioned by God* (Genesis 1:26); 2) *Made in the image of God out of the dust of the earth* (Genesis 2:7); 3) *Washing Instructions:* "Arise, and be baptized, and wash away your sins, calling on His name" (Acts 22:16, NAS); Tumble dry in "the Spirit, and you will not carry out the desire of the flesh" (Galatians 5:16, NAS); 4) *Custom-made:* a) "For whom He foreknew, He also predestined to become conformed to the image of His Son" (Romans 8:29, NAS); b) "For we are His workmanship, created in Christ Jesus for good works, which God prepared beforehand, that we should walk in them" (Ephesians 2:10, NAS).

An old Scotch farmer, looking at a little wild flower under the microscope for the very first time, was awed into silence. When he recovered his speech, he solemnly said, "I would have never stepped on it, if I had known it was so beautiful!"

If we would only spend more time viewing ourselves, our creation and our recreation, under the microscope of God's Word, we, too, would say in the words of the old Scotch farmer, "I would have never stepped on myself if I had known *I* was so beautiful, nor would I have allowed another person to crush me beneath the weight of his foot!"

Let's take another look at those three songs we couldn't sing and see if we can't look at things from God's perspective.

The words of the first song were taken from

Psalm 139:14, (NAS), "I will give thanks to Thee, for I am fearfully and wonderfully made."

You know, it's amazing how we can get all wrapped up in our facial features and body measurements and completely miss the wonder and the beauty of our creation. The very fact of our existence, in any size or shape, should make us want to bow the knee and give thanks and glory to God!

In *The Medusa and the Snail,* Lewis Thomas, in contemplating the common union of a sperm and egg in that process which ultimately produces a human being, cries out: "The mere existence of that cell should be one of the greatest astonishments of the earth. People ought to be walking around all day, all through their waking hours, calling to each other in endless wonderment, talking of nothing except that cell.... If anyone does succeed in explaining it, within my lifetime, I will charter a skywriting airplane, maybe a whole fleet of them, and send them aloft to write one great exclamation point after another, around the whole sky, until all my money runs out."[2]

I'm sure we would be amused and amazed if we saw a woman open her Bible to the Psalms and read, "The heavens are telling of the glory of God; And their expanse is declaring the work of His hands" (Psalm 19:1, NAS),and then heard her exclaim, "Hold it! It all has to be measured before we can say it is true!" Imagine her reserving judgment on the Psalmist's words until she could personally board a rocket, fly off into outer space, and measure the distance between the sun and the moon, the moon and the stars, and the distance between the stars! Her measurements would prove nothing! God has already pronounced His judgment on His own creation, and He has called it "good." And His judgments "are true; they are righteous altogether" (Psalm 19:9, NAS).

Even so, when God stooped down and scooped up the dust of the earth and fashioned man and woman, He said that His creation was "good." All of the tape measures and all of the bathroom scales in the world won't change that! Now it is good that we should want to take care of our bodies through wholesome eating, adequate exercise, and rest. Writes the apostle Paul, "Or do you not know that your body is a temple of the Holy Spirit who is in you, whom you have from God, and that you are not your own? For you have been bought with a price: therefore glorify God in your body" (1 Corinthians 6:19, 20, NAS). But beyond a healthy concern for your body, I beg of you, get your mind off your measurements. You are not your measurements! You are a child of God!

Concerning the size and shape of the human body, even humanly speaking, there is no universal ideal. In one Oriental culture, for instance, it is considered good that people should be as inconspicuous as possible. This philosophy carries over to the extent that it is good for a woman to be flat-chested so she will not be noticed. In fact, one of the greatest compliments that a boy in this culture can give a girl is to say, "You are so beautiful you are just like everyone else!" In our Western culture, by contrast, you know the philosophy. The bosom is emphasized. What is the perfect figure supposed to be—36-24-36? I believe those are the devil's measurements to keep women in a constant state of dissatisfaction with themselves. God loves variety! He has made all kinds of body types. I used to exercise at Spa Lady in Cincinnati, and I saw those body types. There are just some things about our bodies that all of the dieting and all of the exercising in the world won't change!

If you are struggling over the way God made you, or if there is even one thing about yourself that you are having trouble accepting, I can identify with that. But we've got to get beyond our pain caused by worldly concepts of beauty or our own personal preferences, and get into the reality of life as it was meant to be lived in Jesus Christ.

I have five children. If you were to ask me which of the five is the most beautiful, I would just look at you and shake my head in astonishment. I'm their mother! They're all beautiful! If you were to ask God which of His children is the most beautiful, I can imagine His looking at you in amazement and saying, "I'm their Father! They're all beautiful!"

Let's turn now to the second song we couldn't sing: "I am the vine, you are the branches; he who abides in Me, and I in him, he bears much fruit" (John 15:5, NAS).

Your body has "fingerprints" that match no other person's in the world. No one else in all of the world has a mind that's just like your mind. No one else in all of the world has a heart that's just like your heart. No one else in all of the world has a personality that's just like your personality. Even though other people have some of the same gifts you have, by the time these gifts are processed through *your* mind, *your* heart, and *your* personality, they become a unique gift to God and to man that will never ever be duplicated by anyone else in all of the world for all of time! You have no double!

Rejoice over the gifts you see in others. God put them there not only to bless them, but to bless you and to fill up that which is lacking in your life. Then look inside yourself to discover the wonderful gifts that God has given to you. Rejoice over them, even as you rejoice over the gifts of others, and use them to His glory.

We turn now to that third song we couldn't conscientiously sing: "There is therefore now no condemnation for those who are in Christ Jesus" (Romans 8:1, NAS).

I think one of the most pathetic scenes in all of history must be that of Adam and Eve nestled together in the garden holding fig leaves to cover themselves. Their bodies were perfect, beautifully formed by the hand of God himself. But self-esteem has to do with more than our bodies. It has to do with our souls. This is one reason why I believe the whole area of self-esteem becomes such a critical issue in the teenage years. At that time boys and girls are not only experiencing awesome changes as they mature physically and emotionally; they are also experiencing awesome changes as they mature as spiritual beings and reach the age of accountability and realize that their souls are standing naked before their Maker.

When Adam and Eve sinned, they started looking for fig leaves. Ever after, we have been looking for fig leaves—appearance, performance, status—to cover our lost self-esteem.

My heart breaks when I think of God patiently making garments of skin for Adam and Eve so they could be clothed. He has done far more than this for all of us. As Isaiah cries out, "I will rejoice greatly in the Lord, My soul will exult in my God; For He has clothed me with garments of salvation, He has wrapped me with a robe of righteousness, As a bridegroom decks himself with a garland, And as a bride adorns herself with her jewels" (Isaiah 61:10, NAS).

If you are a child of God and remain faithful unto death, this wedding invitation is for you:

The Father
requests the honour of your presence
at the marriage supper of His Son
Jesus Christ
to be held in Heaven.
Only those will be admitted
who come clothed in the Wedding Garment
provided by the Father.
The Spirit and the bride say, "Come!"[3]

---

[1]Adapted from J. Chapman Bradley's story, "The Angel Who Refused to Sing," December, 1943. Used by permission of *The Presbyterian Outlook,* 512 E. Main St., Richmond, VA 23219.

[2]Lewis Thomas, *The Medusa and the Snail* (New York: Viking Penguin Inc., 1979), pp. 155-157. Reprinted by permission of Viking Penguin Inc.

[3]Taken off the cover of an album, "In The Spirit Of The Bride," by Marilou recorded at Superior Sound Studios, Hendersonville, Tennessee. Used by permission.

Watering the Flower of Self-Esteem

One day outside my window
I saw a mockingbird.
She stood in modest costume
preening her ashgray feathers,
her long slender body
silhouetted against
new-fallen snow
and the deep green of fern.

I could not detect
one feather out of place,
but I watched her carefully
as she kept arranging
and rearranging her coat.
Occasionally, she pressed
her beak deep within
in order to smooth out feathers
that were hidden from view.
It mattered not that
others could not see them.
She knew they were there,
nestled against her warm body.
And she cared for them as tenderly
as she cared for her outer coat
that received the caressing
of the winter's winds.

She stopped her busy work a moment
and cocked her eye at me,
seeming to study me.
Seeing my deep look of approval,
she lifted her voice in song.

Then she lowered her head again,
tilting it to one side
as she eyed me carefully.
Inspired by my full acceptance of her,
she left off mimicking other birds
and produced a melody of her own—
a rare song of beauty and joy.

Gain Heart by

Surmounting Grief

If you look down on a cloud, it's a useless mass—
totally nonsupportive and unproductive.
But if you look up to a cloud, it will send
its rain and cause your flowers to blossom.

It is deeply comforting to me to remember that the principles of all successful psychology may be found in the Bible. They lie there in varying depths simply waiting for men of faith to dig them out. For in Him "are hidden all the treasures of wisdom and knowledge" (Colossians 2:3, NAS).

For example, thousands of years ago our heavenly Father, being filled with love and compassion for man, revealed to him the five currently proposed and now widely accepted stages of grief: 1) *denial and isolation;* 2) *anger;* 3) *depression;* 4) *bargaining;* and 5) *acceptance.* This particular discovery was unearthed in the book of Job.

Job's initial reaction to grief was nothing less than awe-inspiring. Bereft of children and possessions, Job knelt before his Maker and said, "Naked I came from my mother's womb, And naked I shall return there. The Lord gave and the Lord has taken away. Blessed be the name of the Lord" (Job 1:21, NAS).

In full acceptance of God's dealings with him, Job thrust aside the first four stages of grief—momentarily. Then his sorrow began to churn within him until, finally, he opened his mouth and cursed the day of his birth. In the heated dialogues that followed, Job aimed his words like arrows at the target of self-defense. Much later, we find Job back down on his knees, crying to his Maker, "Behold, I am insignificant; what can I reply to Thee? I lay my hand on my mouth. Once I have spoken, and I will not answer; Even twice, and I will add no more" (Job 40:4, 5, NAS).

What took place between chapters three and forty of Job? The German theologian, Dietrich Bonhoeffer, once said, "When Christ calls a man, he bids him come and die."[1] To put it simply, Job was crucified.

Job entered into the deepest denial humanly possible save for the denial of God himself. He was preoccupied with denying his cross instead of denying himself.

I'm reminded of a night long ago. LaVerne and I were living in a bamboo and grass house in a Rawang tribal village in northern Burma. Marcia, our firstborn, was one year old. On this particular night, LaVerne was away from home. Marcia and I were settled down for the night when, all of a sudden, I was awakened by the sound of bells and knew that some horses had found their way into our grounds. They were never welcome because they ate the vegetation and trampled it underfoot. Since LaVerne was gone, I hastened outside, called our dog, Pepper, picked up a long stick, and proceeded to let the invaders know that they were not wanted. (If you were to ask my children, you would find that this is *not* the mental image they have of their mother!)

I ran clear to the end of the enclosed fields a little distance from the house and started toward the jungle to the back of us to try to make the horses run in the direction of the open front gate. Suddenly, I thought about the tigers that roamed in the area and their fondness for traveling in bright moonlight! I promptly turned on my heels and dashed madly for home, the bottoms of my flannel pajamas flapping wildly beneath a hurriedly-put-on skirt!

As I snuggled into bed again, I thought how funny the whole incident would have appeared to an onlooker as there had been no visible cause for my wild scramble back home.

We all know what it means to be preoccupied with the "horses"—those sorrows that invade our grounds and trample our lives underfoot. But we must remember that while we are preoccupied with the "horses," the devil is roaming the jungle behind our houses seeking whom he may devour! We need to stop chasing the "horses" and flee back to the safety of the will of God—our only sure house of refuge.

God doesn't cause everything to happen that happens in our lives, because the devil is alive and well on planet Earth. But by the time something reaches us, it has either passed through His directive will or His permissive will. Of this one thing you may be sure—He's aiming to get glory out of it! As Peter said, "In this you greatly rejoice, though now for a little while you may have had to suffer grief in all kinds of trials. These have come so that your faith—of greater worth than gold, which perishes even though refined by fire—may be proved genuine and may result in praise, glory and honor when Jesus Christ is revealed" (1 Peter 1:6, 7, New International Version).

There's something very special about you because of the things God has led you through. There's a very special ministry that you have to perform that no one else can perform because of the things God has led you through. "Be on the alert. Your adversary, the devil, prowls about like a roaring lion, seeking someone to devour. But resist him, firm in your faith, knowing that the same experiences of suffering are being accomplished by your brethren who are in the world" (1 Peter 5:8, 9, NAS).

How can we walk victoriously through this first stage of grief and through the succeeding stages of grief into the final stage of full acceptance? I believe we can do it by seeing how Jesus endured His cross. "For we do not have a high priest who cannot sympathize with our weaknesses, but one who has been tempted in all things as we are, yet without sin. Let us therefore draw near with confidence to the throne of grace, that we may receive mercy and may find grace to help in time of need" (Hebrews 4:15, 16, NAS).

Denial and Isolation

The apostle John tells us that Jesus "went out, bearing His own cross, to the place called the Place of a Skull, which is called in Hebrew, Golgatha" (John 19:17, NAS). Matthew, Mark, and Luke record that the men who led Christ out to crucify Him "pressed into service a passer-by coming from the country, Simon of Cyrene (the father of Alexander and Rufus), to bear His cross" (Mark 15:21, NAS). This suggests that Jesus staggered and fell beneath the weight of the cross at the city gate, and from that point on His cross had to be carried by another.

Do you feel you can't carry the weight of your cross? Christ understands! Perhaps that's why He said, "Bear one another's burdens, and thus fulfill the law of Christ" (Galatians 6:2, NAS). There are times in our lives when we need at least one other person to carry the full weight of our crosses in order to make it through the first stage of grief. Whenever we experience this need, we may come to the throne of grace to ask for His special providential care, fully assured that He understands and cares. We also need to do what is humanly possible by seeking out those whom we think might be able to bear our burdens and share our loads. Having done this, it is best for us to leave the final choice of crossbearer with Him. For we do not know the hearts of men, as does our Lord. In our humanness we may try to force others to minister to us who really are not able to carry our crosses—not because they do not love us and not because they do not love the Lord, but because they are already carrying other heavy burdens. We must also have the courage to await God's timing in the matter. It may differ from ours.

Anger

When our Lord lay down on the cross and the executioners were ready to hammer the nails into His hands, He offered no resistance! "He was oppressed and afflicted, yet he did not open his mouth; he was led like a lamb to the slaughter, and as a sheep before her shearers is silent, so he did not open his mouth" (Isaiah 53:7, New International Version).

When some deep grief comes to us, we are often afraid of experiencing it and use all of our energy to fight it off. What we need to do is to lie down on our crosses and fully relax our hands, opening our palms to God while we willingly take in, through His grace and strength, the pain that has come to us until it reaches a deep psychological level. We may need to go through this exercise a hundred times for full healing—even lying down on the floor and visualizing ourselves going through this hammering stage if necessary. When we do, and when we ask God not for a reduced measure of pain, but for an increased measure of grace, we will receive solace beyond all our imagining. If we have been wronged, we will be able to cry out with Christ, "Father, forgive them; for they know not what they do" (Luke 23:34).

Because Christ was unencumbered with personal anger, He was able to reach out to the thief on the cross and minister to his needs. When you and I are blinded by our rage, we can't even see our brother hanging on the cross next to us, much less minister to him. When our anger cools, and we reach out to our brother, we will experience further healing.

Depression

Jesus did not hang on the cross and mourn for former days when palm branches were strewn before Him as He rode triumphantly into Jerusalem. He simply busied himself with the task at hand: "When Jesus therefore saw his mother, and the disciple standing by, whom he loved, he saith unto his mother, Woman, behold thy son! Then saith he to the disciple, Behold thy mother!" (John 19:26, 27).

Then Jesus must have been tempted to enter into a state of depression unknown to man as He cried out, "My God, my God, why hast thou forsaken me?" (Matthew 27:46) From all appearances, the cry went unheeded. Then Jesus said simply, "I thirst" (John 19:28). "And straightway one of them ran, and took a sponge, and filled it with vinegar, and put it on a reed, and gave him to drink? (Matthew 27:48).

Christ did not push the sponge away from His parched lips crying, "If You aren't going to give Me what I long for most of all, I don't want anything at all!" Though His deepest cry was for union and communion with His heavenly Father, He humbled himself in the midst of God's dealings with Him. Following the stark silence from Heaven, He simply lowered His head and with His parched mouth sucked on a sponge filled with vinegar. Vinegar instead of union!

Sometimes when you and I are depressed, we are dissatisfied with everything in life because the deepest longing of our hearts has not been answered. Going through life concentrating on what we don't have instead of on what we do have is like going through life "singing" the rests of a song instead of the notes! God gives us "the garment of praise for the spirit of heaviness" (Isaiah 61:3). When this cloak of praise is thrown around our shoulders and we stand in total darkness before our Maker "sucking on a sponge filled with vinegar," our humble acceptance of His dealings with us becomes a special act of praise and worship—precious to God and rare among men.

Bargaining

There were no "ifs" in Christ's relationship with God. He had a job to do—a death to die. And He did it! And when it was over, He simply said, "It is finished" (John 19:30).

I remember a time back in 1957. It was the beginning of the monsoon season when air service to Putao, the airstrip close to us, was to be suspended. I had a throbbing toothache! Due to the kindness of the Army personnel, I was able to fly to Rangoon on an Army plane. But on the return trip, flying United Burma Airways, I could fly back only as far north as Myitkyina. From there I joined a party of travelers and journeyed by jeep a distance of one hundred and thirty-two miles to the village of Sumprabum. The last eighty or so miles had to be covered by foot. Coming to the close of one particularly difficult day, I sighted the government bungalow where our party was to rest for the night. Approaching the bungalow, I walked slowly up the steps, across the front room into one of the rooms which contained a bedstead, and stretched out on the hard "mattress"—completely exhausted. Toward evening I reached out for some spiritual food, and what blessed strength I found in the particular selection I chose. Included was this illustration:

"In the Franco-Prussian war a gunner was commanded by his colonel to fire on a small house which sheltered a number of Prussians. With pale face the gunner obeyed. He sighted his piece deliberately and accurately, and then fired. 'Well hit, my man,' said the officer as he looked through his glass. 'That cottage could not have been very strong, it is completely smashed.' As he turned around, he noticed a tear on the gunner's cheek. 'Why, what's the matter?' he exclaimed roughly. 'Pardon me, Colonel,' was the answer. 'It was my own little home—everything I had in the world.' ... Let Calv'ry's rays so atomize my every nest where slackness lies, that 'breaking peace with compromise, to sacrificial heights I rise!'"

Acceptance

Christ drank the cup of suffering down to the last dregs. Then He said, "Father, into thy hands I commend my spirit" (Luke 23:46).

> "Wherefore God also hath highly exalted him, and given him a name which is above every name: that at the name of Jesus every knee should bow, of things in heaven, and things in earth, and things under the earth; And that every tongue should confess that Jesus Christ is Lord, to the glory of God the Father."
>
> (Philippians 2:9-11)
>
> "Wherefore let them that suffer according to the will of God commit the keeping of their souls to him in well doing, as unto a faithful Creator."
>
> (1 Peter 4:19)

------

[1]Dietrich Bonhoeffer, *The Cost of Discipleship* (New York: The Macmillan Company, 1949) p. 8.

Sorrow Touched Me

Sorrow touched me yesterday—
not with a
light,
deft stroke of her fingers,
but with an icy clutch.
Without warning
the damp,
raw winds of winter
penetrated
every fiber of my being.
My eyes could no more reject
the tears that came
unbeckoned
than winter could reject
the early morning frost.

Someone passing by
did not understand the nature of
tears
and frost.
And drawing his "spiritual" robes
around him,
he stopped long enough
to stand
on the sidelines of my life
and quote Scriptures on
joy
before moving on.
My soul was so bowed with grief
I did not see him depart.

Then one day someone else
entered my life.
Upon seeing my tears,
straightway,
tears welled up
in my sister's eyes.
And she thought
not of Scriptures to admonish,
but of our human predicament!
And she sat down beside me
and wept.
And when we had finished weeping,
we talked together
of the Lord and His ways.
And behold,
the early morning sun
dispelled the frost from our hearts.
And we arose
and went our separate ways—
rejoicing.

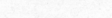

Gain Heart by

Resolving Marital Conflict

To go through life looking for love is to
squander life. To spend one's love looking
for life is to find it.

Prologue

With slowness and deliberation, Sandy pulled out all of the stops in the organ of her soul. Feel she must. She studied her husband who was leaning against the railing of the ship as they cruised in the moonlight. She felt longing—the kind of painful longing that fills a woman when she is aware of dreams yet unfulfilled. For years she had prayed for the gift of Eros for this man—for the flame of the Lord as mentioned in the book of Solomon. "Love is as strong as death, Jealousy is as severe as Sheol; Its flashes are flashes of fire, The very flame of the Lord. Many waters cannot quench love, Nor will rivers overflow it; If a man were to give all the riches of his house for love, It would be utterly despised" (Song of Solomon 8:6, 7, NAS).

The light cast by the moon on the waters shed an unearthly beauty on the landscape around them. "Father," she cried. "It isn't Cupid who shoots those arrows. It's You! And Your quiver is full! Why can't You shoot just one of them through my heart for my husband? It would take so little effort on Your part. It's been years since I first asked You." Her tears made their way reverently from the labyrinth of grief deep within her to an uncharted world without. She had tried to kill this dream of hers a thousand times. But some force within her, like the relentless tide of the sea, kept driving her back to the shores of her longings. Oh, God, she had tried to give it up, but the very thought made life insipid to her—a tasteless affair with no meaning—a life she did not even want to contemplate.

She began to study the movement of the waters below, as though in them she could discover the answers she needed. Suddenly, she felt the Lord's arrow piercing her heart! Trembling, she lifted her face to John. The emotion was so fierce it was like bands of steel compared with the soft threads that had first united her with this man. She thought those threads were so strong then. In fact, she did not even encounter the thought of marrying any other man. Her love for John, her desire for him was settled in her soul long before his lips ever proposed or she had verbalized her feelings to him or to herself. She was a child then—not mature enough for the gift of Eros. She did not even know how to handle those threads of longing that were hers.

John stood there, his arm resting on the railing of the ship. He looked at her kindly—having no knowledge of the events transpiring in her soul. In a moment she was in his embrace. She could not believe the wonder of it--that it was happening to her! She longed to be one with this man who had been an enigma for so many years. They returned to their cabin below.

The morning rays of sunlight tugged playfully at Sandy's eyelids. She opened them slowly, feeling a joy and peace in her soul she could not describe. Then, with a start, she realized that she was in her own bedroom and not on board ship! She looked at John still sleeping beside her. Slowly and deliberately she shoved back all of the stops in the organ of her soul and pulled the organ lid over the keys. Her struggle began anew.

A Reason for Hope

We live in a society whose theme songs are "love" and "marriage," and those songs are being sung "loud and clear" not only by the non-Christian world, but by the Christian world as well. In fact, we can hardly turn around—even within our own homes—without being touched or influenced by the philosophies of both worlds.

With all the deluge of material, both written and vocal, it is sometimes difficult for us to remember that the ultimate purpose for our existence is not marriage. Jesus said, "The sons of this age marry and are given in marriage, but those who are considered worthy to attain to that age and the resurrection from the dead, neither marry, nor are given in marriage; for neither can they die anymore, for they are like angels, and are sons of God, being sons of the resurrection" (Luke 20:34-36, NAS). We were not made for marriage. Marriage was made for us. We were made for Jesus Christ: "For by Him all things were created, both in the heavens and on earth, visible and invisible, whether thrones or dominions or rulers or authorities—all things have been created by Him and for Him" (Colossians 1:16, NAS).

What, then, is the ultimate purpose for our existence in this temporary world? The apostle John answers the question with eloquence when he writes, "And I heard, as it were, the voice of a great multitude and as the sound of many waters and as the sound of mighty peals of thunder, saying, 'Hallelujah! For the Lord our God, the Almighty, reigns. Let us rejoice and be glad and give the glory to Him, for the marriage of the Lamb has come and His bride has made herself ready'" (Revelation 19:6, 7, NAS).

We live, we breathe to prepare ourselves and others for the wedding banquet of the Lamb. We make ourselves ready by placing ourselves in the role of the bride and becoming Christlike. We make others ready by placing ourselves in the role of the bridesmaid and helping them as they prepare for their heavenly wedding day. We do this by being full of good works on their behalf, especially at the point of our spiritual gifts. We were destined for both roles from the foundation of the world:

> "For whom He foreknew, He also predestined to become conformed to the image of His Son."
>
> (Romans 8:29, NAS)

> "For we are His workmanship, created in Christ Jesus for good works, which God prepared beforehand, that we should walk in them."
>
> (Ephesians 2:10, NAS)

e were also destined to find our wholeness in Christ.
in Him all the fulness of Deity dwells in bodily form,
.... in Him you have been made complete" (Colossians 2:9, 10, NAS).

We find wholeness not in another person, even a male counterpart, but in Christ, and in all of the experiences and relationships which God brings to bear upon us as He conforms us to the image of His Son. We err when we refer, however lovingly, to a mate's "better half." The Scriptural equation, the mystery of the marriage union, is not that $\frac{1}{2} + \frac{1}{2} = 1$, but that $1 + 1 = 1$. Often the challenge to a marriage is that two people are being brought together who are looking for wholeness in each other and who have not yet had sufficient time to reach their maturity in Christ. But God, who makes "all things to work together for good to those who love God" (Romans 8:28, NAS), uses this fragile union itself to aid the maturation process. To dissolve a union because there are problems, even severe ones, is to bypass one of God's marvelous plans for perfecting us in Christ. As my father once said, "The Christian has a struggle because he is a Christian." Hopefully, as time progresses, and as we cooperate with God, our relationships will become more an expression of our wholeness than a means to it until our life-style is basically the same on both sides of the grave.

All of this emphasis on the eternal does not minimize the importance of earthly marriage. To the contrary, it places marriage within its proper framework thereby elevating her joys, alleviating her sorrows, and bridging the need to be married in order to experience wholeness and fullness of life. Neither does viewing marriage from an eternal perspective encourage asceticism, a "self-made religion and self-abasement and severe treatment of the body" (Colossians 2:23, NAS) strongly condemned by the apostle Paul. Nowhere is this taught in the Scriptures as a pathway to happiness or a means of pleasing God. I personally grieve over Buddha's desertion of his wife and baby so he could go out into the world to "find truth."

This is in direct contrast to the spirit of Christ, who challenges a man in his quest for God, to go deeper and deeper into his relationship with his wife until he learns to love her "just as Christ also loved the church and gave Himself up for her" (Ephesians 5:25, NAS).

In the scene following the great sea battle in the movie, *Ben-Hur,* Judah Ben-Hur and Arrius, the tribune, were adrift on a plank a short distance from the flaming ships. Judah had saved Arrius from drowning, but Arrius wanted to kill himself. As became a Roman tribune, he desired to go down with his ship in the midst of the foe rather than submit to dishonor. "Why did you save me?" he cried. Whereupon Judah, remembering the words that Arrius had spoken to the galley slaves who were chained to their oars, mimicked him, saying, "We keep you alive to serve this ship. Row well and live!"

If we are not grounded in the eternal and we run up against problems in our marriages and see our ships of matrimony beginning to sink, we, too, like Arrius, may want to reach out for something to put an end to it all. It doesn't have to be a knife. Most of us don't commit suicide. It doesn't even have to be divorce. We may simply grab hold of something marked "self-destruct" and pursue it to its bitter end: overeating, overwork, withdrawal, worry, bitterness, or the like. We may even cry out to the Lord as Arrius cried to Judah, "Why did You save me?"

God doesn't keep any of us alive to serve the ship of some sick matrimony. He keeps us alive so that through our marriages, and whatever else life may present to us, we may continually prepare ourselves and others for our heavenly wedding day. As the Scriptures say, "His bride has made herself ready." To divorce ourselves from our mates for unscriptural reasons is to frustrate the plan of God. It's like getting an abortion when God is in the midst of fashioning something beautiful!

Some Problems Involved

Here is a word on marriage from the secular world by Otto Dekom of Gannett News Service:

"Live-in lovers are out. Marriage is in. The reason is that a live-in relationship lacks commitment—the essential ingredient of a permanent relationship. Living together proves nothing, because it does not involve the restrictions, problems and adjustments of real marriage.

"'The pendulum,' said Dr. Walter W. Brackelmanns, a psychiatrist, 'is swinging.

"'There was a time when living together was in style. People believed that they could work through all those psychological problems of marriage in advance. What happened was that the young people found out that it doesn't work.

"'From the time you get married, the whole ball game changes. It's as if you had never lived together. . . .

"'I think there are too many divorces. Things need to be done to find ways to deal with this epidemic. There are 6,000 marriages a day and 3,000 divorces.' . . ."[1]

So the world, in the process of ignoring God, swings from one fad to another in its never-ending search for the fountain of truth.

Why are two people incompatible? The excuses are legion—the reasons one:

They thought they were incompatible,
that their personalities just didn't blend—
through no fault of their own, of course!
It was just one of those things that happens sometimes,
and this time it happened to them!
Therefore, they genuinely felt
the responsibility for their relationship
lay somewhere outside themselves.
After all, she was Sanquine-Melancholy,
and he was Choleric-Phlegmatic.
And what else can you expect
from a combination like that?
But really, it was just that
their weaknesses were incompatible.
Because when God fills two people with His Spirit,
no matter what their temperaments,
they make beautiful music together.

I know God enjoys the angel songs.
In fact, if I were He,
I'd be strongly tempted to sit back on my throne
and satisfy myself with the music of Heaven
instead of subjecting my ears
to the jangled discords of men.
But not God!
I can see Him bending down every single minute

92

to catch some heavenly strains
from the Planet Earth!

Oh, Lord, help us, Your children,
no matter what our temperaments
or situations
to make beautiful music—
not just for our own selfish enjoyment,
but for **You!**

What do you do when the pain of your union is insupportable despite the fact that, ideally, you and your husband should be making beautiful music together?

There are several options—not all of them Christian. For example, quoting the newspaper article with which I began, Dr. Walter W. Brackelmanns "compares marriage to a living organism, which 'has a birth, a developmental period and a death. It is always in flux and transition. The two people in marriage are always changing and, hopefully growing—and, therefore, their relationship is always changing.'

"Brackelmanns considers most of the counseling ordered by courts during and after divorce to be wasteful and useless.

"'You can do horrible things to a marriage, and it will survive. But there is a point of no return and when it appears, the marriage is dead. The critical thing is that people must have their consciousness raised so they don't reach the point of no return, that they solve problems in time.'"[2]

Is there a point of no return in marriage for the Christian? What do you do when love is gone?

A Look at Some Options

Marriage failure is more than a legal statistic. It's people hurting. It's people broken. It's people—sometimes reaching out, sometimes striking out, not knowing where to turn.

Few of us handle great pain and loss with ease. Some, not knowing how else to cope, take an ascetic approach and turn against marriage in the name of spirituality. Some time ago my mother took me on a trip to Shakertown, Kentucky. As we began our tour of this early Shaker settlement, one of the first things that attracted my attention was a statement of beliefs displayed for public view: "Perhaps the most misunderstood tenet of Shakerism and the cause of derision and often persecution from 'The World' was the Believers' concurrence with the proscription of Mother Ann requiring each member of the Society to lead the life of a celibate. Mother Ann's doctrine was simple: Confession was the door to the regenerate life, celibacy its rule and cross. Deceitful wantonness of both male and female was at the root of hatred, envy, jealousy, and murder among individuals and of destruction and war among nations. If passions were not overcome in this world they would become more powerful in the world of the Spirit."

Why did Mother Ann Lee feel so strongly about the need to divorce marriage from genuine spirituality? As has been said of Augustine, Pelagius and Francis of Assisi, her psychological dictates probably stemmed from the circumstances of her life. Posted close to the statement of beliefs was another placard giving facts about Mother Ann Lee's personal life. She was born in Manchester, England, on February 29, 1736, one of eight children of an illiterate blacksmith. "A wretched marriage and the death of her four children in infancy drove the young woman to fervid participation in the activities of the newly-formed Shaker group, and in 1772 she assumed its leadership with the title of Mother. A mystical experience had persuaded her that she was the Messiah, returned to show men the way to salvation through abstinence, good works, and industry."

One of the most successful ways we can ruin our lives and the lives of those around us is to allow a root of bitterness to spring up within us and give it a religious twist "to the glory of God." Shakerism is an extreme example of asceticism. However, asceticism may also find expression within the framework of marriage. It manifests itself in a myriad of ways ranging from subtle, unconscious attitudes within the husband or wife to dramatic episodes between them revealing nonacceptance of their marital state. Whatever its expression may be, asceticism is the exact antithesis of the spirit of Christ, who exaulted marriage to such a degree that He used it to symbolize His love for the church and the church's love for Him: "Husbands, love your wives, just as Christ also loved the church and gave Himself up for her . . .

and let the wife see to it that she respect her husband"
(Ephesians 5:25, 33, NAS).

Some who would never consider the ascetic approach
may attempt to handle their pain and loss by shifting the
whole burden of their problems onto the Lord. I recall a
story written by Kahlil Gibran which comes out of the context of Eastern culture at a time when marriage brokers
mercilessly imposed marriage in which love was not
present. In Gibran's story Wardeh Al Haneh was forced to
marry Rashid Nu'man. She laments: "I prayed in the silence
of the nights before Heaven, asking it to create in my soul a
spiritual affinity that would draw close to me the man who
had been chosen for my husband. But Heaven did not do so,
for love descends on our spirits on God's command and not
on man's asking. Then one black day I looked beyond the
darkness and saw a soft light shining from the eyes of a
youth who walked the highways of life alone and who dwelt
alone among his books and papers in this poor house. I
closed my eyes that I might not see those rays, and said
within myself: 'Thy lot, O spirit, is the blackness of the
tomb; covet not, therefore, the light!'"[3] When she fled from
the husband who had been forced upon her, Wardeh felt that
she was being led by a sacred and divine force.

Shall we pray as Wardeh prayed—howbeit within a
Christian context—asking God to dissolve our problems and
then, if the answers we covet do not descend upon us with
the swiftness and sureness of "Cupid's arrows," resign ourselves to a life of unhappiness or leave our husbands?
Neither reflects the spirit of Christ who admonished us,
"Wives, be submissive to your own husbands so that even if
any of them are disobedient to the word, they may be won
without a word by the behavior of their wives, as they ob-
serve your chaste and respectful behavior. And let not your
adornment be merely external—braiding the hair, and wearing gold jewelry, or putting on dresses; but let it be the
hidden person of the heart, with the imperishable quality of
a gentle and quiet spirit, which is precious in the sight of
God" (1 Peter 3:1-4, NAS).

When one option after another is closed, a woman who is
involved in a very difficult or unsatisfying relationship with
her husband may suffer from a hemmed-in feeling. She
must remember that she is not alone. Even Christ's disciples

felt a kind of deep despair when they listened to Christ's teaching on marriage:

> "And some Pharisees came to Him, testing Him, and saying, 'Is it lawful for a man to divorce his wife for any cause at all?' And He answered and said, "Have you not read, that He who created them from the beginning made them male and female, and said, 'For this cause a man shall leave his father and mother, and shall cleave to his wife; and the two shall become one flesh'? Consequently they are no longer two, but one flesh. What therefore God has joined together, let no man separate." They said to Him, 'Why then did Moses command to give her a certificate and divorce her?' He said to them, "Because of your hardness of heart, Moses permitted you to divorce your wives; but from the beginning it has not been this way. And I say to you, whoever divorces his wife, except for immorality, and marries another woman commits adultery."
>
> (Matthew 19:3-9, NAS)

Christ's disciples understood the difficulty of looking at marriage from God's point of view for they replied, "If the relationship of the man with his wife is like this, it is better not to marry" (Matthew 19:10, NAS).

The problems within each marriage are as common and as unique as every snowflake. To deal with every possible option or problem from the Christian and non-Christian points of view is far beyond the scope of this writing. It is my desire at this time to focus in on the problems of a woman who has fallen out of love with her husband. What can a bride—whether she be twenty or fifty—once so in love, now with love gone, do when the pain of her union becomes insupportable? Is there light at the end of the dark tunnel? Oh, yes, there is light—a light so dazzling it brings us to our knees before Christ, "in whom are hidden all the treasures of wisdom and knowledge" (Colossians 2:3, NAS).

An Option in Christ

How do we fall in and out of love? I realize some will object to this terminology, insisting that we "grow in love." However, if we refrain from using it, we will simply need to invent some other expression to say the same thing. As my husband once said to me, "If there is no falling in love, what happened to me when I saw you?"

The mysterious phenomenon of falling in love has existed since the dawn of time. To erase this experience as having nothing to do with love is to deny the many God-given kinds and levels of love—insisting, I believe unfortunately, that love must be reduced to "one thing."

How do we fall out of love? This is not nearly so mysterious a phenomenon as falling in love. It is true that we may fall out of love for no conscious reason. It is likewise true that we may fall out of love owing to a forced separation, causing our initial feelings never to be given an opportunity for adequate expression and growth. A potential for a deep love may also die voluntarily because we know we cannot nurture the kind of love we feel and honor God at the same time. But if we have loved another sufficiently to go through a serious courtship, and if we have then walked down the aisle and committed our lives "for better for worse," it is likely, if we have fallen out of love, that we have done so by unconsciously disregarding, in their God-given sequence, laws as immutable as the law of gravity. Let me put the matter in story form:

Tom and Susan fell in love. God's blessing was upon their love. They were united in Christ and were deeply devoted to Him in every way. Their feelings registered *nine* on a scale from one to nine.

But Susan fell into god-playing by exalting her relationship with Tom above God, who created and designed the gift of Eros. To her, "being in love" was everything. Her feelings fell to *eight* on a scale from one to nine.

Then, instead of repenting and repositioning her joy under God, she descended still further into god-playing by elevating Tom inordinately. (All of this god-playing was taking place on an unconscious level, but that it was taking place was evident by the symptoms which followed.) Tom was now not only foremost in her thoughts, but the goal of her existence. Having made him "god," she looked to him to fill all her needs instead of looking to Christ, who alone can fill every need, and freeing Tom to fill whatever needs he could. Her feelings fell to *seven* on a scale from one to nine.

Again, instead of repenting and repositioning Tom under God, acknowledging him as a human being with both weaknesses and strengths, she assumed a demanding spirit. When Tom did not respond to her needs as she dreamed of his responding, she began to question his love. She vacillated between being angry and aloof in her relationship with him. Her feelings fell to *six* on a scale from one to nine.

Then, instead of letting her deep insecurity drive her to Christ and to His answers for her life, she allowed it to feed on pride. When her pride and insecurity were perfectly joined, she conceived hatred in her heart—not only for Tom, but for herself. For her self-worth was wrapped up in Tom instead of in Christ, the Author and Giver of self-worth. Her feelings fell to *five* on a scale from one to nine.

Now, frustrated in her efforts to make Tom "god," she dethroned him and made herself "god" in his place. (Again, this was taking place on an unconscious level.) From this time forward, she puffed up herself against Tom in direct opposition to Christ's command, "Let the wife see to it that she respect her husband" (Ephesians 5:33, NAS). Her feelings fell to *four* on a scale from one to nine.

When this change in strategy didn't work, she became bitter—that state of heart one enters into when one is crying out, "My will, not Thine be done," and God isn't listening. Since she had no faith in Christ's dreams for her, she had no means whereby she could bring her own dreams to fulfillment. Her feelings fell to *three* on a scale from one to nine.

Susan was running out of options, and she knew it. Still, she refused to repent and reposition her dream and herself under God. Instead, she decided to wage an all-out war against Tom in a last-ditch effort to save her marriage. She appointed herself as judge over Tom despite Christ's warning, "Do not judge" (Matthew 7:1, NAS), and she openly pronounced him "guilty." Her feelings fell to *two* on a scale from one to nine.

Since the guilty must suffer punishment, she proceeded to persecute Tom in spite of Christ' command, "Bless and curse not" (Romans 12:14, NAS). Her feelings fell to *one* on a scale from one to nine.

Susan was getting worn out by this time, but she refused to give in. When Tom still would not change, she persecuted him all the more. Her feelings fell to *zero* on a scale from one to nine.

What are Susan's options as a Christian? Is there any promise of Scripture that if a woman falls out of love, as Susan fell out of love with Tom, that she can experience once again the same kind of feelings which accompanied her initial falling in love? For a long time I didn't think so, though I knew Susan could be much happier if she applied Biblical principles to her marriage. I also knew that God could give her the gift of being in love again if He so desired. But I didn't see a promise there. Then I thought of Revelation 2:4, 5, (NAS), *"But I have this against you, that you have left your first love. Remember therefore from where you have fallen, and repent and do the deeds you did at first."*

It is possible to return to a first love. However, we do not fall into it. Rather, we repent and work our way back. Through prayerful study of the Word and observation of mankind, I believe that falling out of love through god-playing is a systematic rejection of the principles taught in the Beatitudes. Christ was not specifically addressing the subject of marriage in the opening of the Sermon on the Mount. However, in mercy and compassion He was revealing in proper sequence the problems we would encounter with feelings and actions when we fashion another "god" and bow down and worship it—be it husband, child, job, or dream.

An Option in Christ Continued

God is the greatest matchmaker in the world. He's all for Eros. He thought it up himself! He meant for it to be a gift— not only to draw us to our mates, but to bless our entire lives. The problem with troubled marriages is not God. The problem is that knowing how to rightly handle His gift is a learning process, and sometimes we lose our way. Let's return now to the story of Susan and Tom.

Susan's cup of torment was now full. No longer able to bear the pain, she found a place for repentance and longed for wholeness more than life. The Commandments, "You shall have no other gods before Me" (Exodus 20:3, NAS) and "You shall love your neighbor as yourself" (Matthew 22:39, NAS), were rigorously obeyed. Though she understandably regressed from time to time, in the main her god-playing ceased.

Now, acknowledging God as "the Judge of all the earth" (Genesis 18:25, NAS) and being in touch not only with her own humanity, but with Tom's humanity as well, she began to identify with his weaknesses instead of persecuting him. Through the process of identification, her judgmental spirit was uprooted, and in its place a spirit of compassion was planted. At this point in time even though she communicated with Tom, when ill-treated, she no longer struck out against him as before. Instead she began to obey the admonition of Scripture, "Never take your own revenge, beloved, but leave room for the wrath of God, for it is written, 'Vengeance is Mine, I will repay,' says the Lord" (Romans 12:19, NAS). But Susan's habits were more deeply embedded than she realized, and she only succeeded in part. However, God honored her efforts. Her feelings rose to *one* on a scale from one to nine.

Encouraged, she persisted in her efforts until all persecution virtually ceased. As she obeyed the Lord's command not to avenge herself, she did so not with a prideful spirit, anxious for God's wrath to fall upon Tom for all of his shortcomings, but with a spirit of humility. For she realized that "there is no partiality with God" (Romans 2:11, NAS) and that in due season she also would receive the Lord's chastening as needed "for those whom the Lord loves He disciplines, and He scourges every son whom He receives" (Hebrews 12:6, NAS). Her feelings rose to *two* on a scale from one to nine.

Then, as the spirit of compassion planted within her grew, it began to yield a harvest of forgiveness. Her sins, which were many, were forgiven her even as Christ promised. Having both offered and received forgiveness, she began to experience "the peace of God, which surpasses all comprehension" (Philippians 4:7, NAS). The long-standing war between Tom and Susan virtually ceased. Her feelings rose to *three* on a scale from one to nine.

Now that Susan was living her life according to Christ's principles, she was making steady progress in her own personal development as well as in her relationship with Tom. The bitterness which had filled her gave way to hope as she watched her dream of loving Tom again coming true. Her faith in Christ deepened, as Christ himself promised it would when He said, "If any man is willing to do His will, he shall know of the teaching, whether it is of God, or whether I speak from myself" (John 7:17, NAS). And faith within her stirred up hope, and hope stirred up love as she responded to the love of God for her. Her feelings rose to *four* on a scale from one to nine.

Though Susan had always been the recipient of God's mercy, she was only now beginning to experience it on a conscious level. In response she began to extend mercy to Tom. This marked the beginning of her deep reaching out to Tom, whereas before she had been preoccupied with his reaching out to her. Now she prayed not for a feeling for Tom, but for a planting of love within her heart that would some day blossom into a love more rare than she had ever felt or known. At this stage of her growth, whereas before she had only been able to refrain from persecuting Tom, she was now capable of going a step further. In so doing she fulfilled the command of Scripture, "Not returning evil for evil, or insult for insult, but giving a blessing instead; for you were called for the very purpose that you might inherit a blessing" (1 Peter 3:9, NAS). Her feelings rose to *five* on a scale from one to nine.

Seeing what a difference Christ made in her life, Susan now hungered and thirsted after righteousness. Christ filled all her needs as He promised He would when He said, "But seek first His kingdom and His righteousness; and all these things shall be added to you" (Matthew 6:33, NAS). As she saw her needs being met, and as she began to successfully exercise control over the sins that had chained her, her inner security and self-esteem grew. As her security and self-esteem grew, little by little the hate that had filled her was abolished. For "perfect love casts out fear" (1 John 4:18, NAS), and what is hate but fear's highest citadel—a walled fortress built to defend oneself. Her feelings rose to *six* on a scale from one to nine.

Now, secure in the knowledge that Christ would provide all her needs, Susan was finally able to release Tom to be what he could be to her. The seed of love planted within her heart took root and grew. Instead of vacillating between being angry and aloof in her relationship with Tom when he did not meet her every need, she began to feel love for him. In time her instinctual need to give passed up her instinctual need to receive. With this change in the balance of things, she was well on her way toward true maturity. She did not turn her back on her genuine needs, which would have been an indication of self-hate. Rather, she yielded them to Christ and concentrated instead on meeting Tom's needs. Her feelings rose to *seven* on a scale from one to nine.

Encouraged, she continued to grow. After months of repenting and following Christ's way, she began to experience in depth the promise of Christ, "Blessed are those who mourn, for they shall be comforted" (Matthew 5:4, NAS). As Christ's comfort filled her life, she began to know the deep serenity which is one of the hallmarks of a mature woman. Her feelings rose to *eight* on a scale from one to nine.

Then she grew deep feelings for the one she fed and cared for. The seed of love which God had planted in her heart came into full bloom.

Epilogue: Susan's love was genuine for her motive in changing was not to manipulate Tom, but to become more beautiful for him, and, with wedding gown in hand, to near the day of her "final fitting" for her heavenly wedding day.

Epilogue

The following lines are shared by way of suggestion, not direction. For you are unique. God will reach down to the level of your sexual needs in His own way and according to His own timetable as you commit your problems and questions to Him. If any thoughts here expressed are helpful, to God be the glory.

* * * * *

The Lord has given you a beautiful body, whatever its size and shape—a garden unique to you filled with all sorts of rare flowers whose blossoms have more to do with the shape of your heart than with the contours of your body. They give off many a sweet fragrance in response to your husband's touch and open into full bloom in response to your deepening acceptance of yourself and your deepening acceptance of him. Unless you are both in a different mood, it is good if you stroll hand in hand down this flower-strewn pathway that leads to the door of your "home" as though time did not exist. For much of life is spent in preparation. Therefore to miss the beauty and the wonder of the time of preparation is to miss the beauty and the wonder of much of life.

This time of joy will grow in harmony and in depth as you both grow emotionally and spiritually and interlace your lives together. Your experience of love will differ from the experience of any other couple in the world, even as your day-by-day communion is unique.

Above the door of your "home" God gave you an exquisite set of door chimes called the clitoris. Your special set of chimes rings differently from any other woman's in the world. For you are unique, and the one who rings your door chimes is unique. God has given you your own special songs with potential built in for playing a variety of themes. These themes will build in harmony and in depth as you grow emotionally and spiritually and interlace your lives together.

Because the chimes vibrate within your "home," your feelings at this time of sharing will be different from those of your lover who caresses you, but God gives to him his own special joy as he enters into the thrill of your music and waits, as a gentleman, for you to open the door.

As he sees you standing there in the doorway and hears you whisper, "May my beloved come into his garden And eat its choice fruits" (Song of Solomon 4:16, NAS), his joy and thanksgiving will know no bounds.

There is neither the need nor the desire to keep standing there ringing the door chimes. For this joy gives way to a still deeper joy only anticipated on the doorstep—the joy of actual union and communion in the inner parlor.

He will reach down into your nature to give of himself to you and to receive sustenance from you. You will give and receive in return—delighting in his highest reaches and praising him for his masculinity and strength, no matter what the level of sharing may be. For his masculinity is a God-given gift he carries within himself always and is not dependent for its existence on his performance on a given day, even as your femininity is a God-given gift you carry within yourself though you vary from day to day in your expression of it. When your mutual love for each other reaches its heights and depths in the sexual expression, the organ chimes will play. As those chimes vibrate, there will be mutual joy. Your joy will grow in harmony and in depth as you grow emotionally and spiritually and interlace your lives together.

If, by night, you make yourself warmly available and express thanks to your husband for his willingness to supply you with his love, he will be filled with a gratitude he will not be able to put into words. And if, by day, you praise him for his determination to supply the world with his needed gifts, he will be inspired to serve mankind with a beauty of purpose that will bring tears to your eyes.

These attitudes will grow in harmony and in depth as you grow emotionally and spiritually and interlace your lives together. Your experience of love will differ from the experience of any other couple in the world, even as your day-by-day communion is unique.

But there are the little foxes. "Catch the foxes for us, The little foxes that are ruining the vineyards, While our vineyards are in blossom" (Song of Solomon 2:15, NAS). In the words of the poet:

"I was asleep, but my heart was awake.
A voice! My beloved was knocking:
'Open to me, my sister, my darling,
My dove, my perfect one!
For my head is drenched with dew,
My locks with the damp of the night.'
"I have taken off my dress,
How can I put it on again?
I have washed my feet,
How can I dirty them again?
"My beloved extended his hand through the opening,
And my feelings were aroused for him.
"I arose to open to my beloved;
And my hands dripped with myrrh,
And my fingers with liquid myrrh,
On the handles of the bolt.
"I opened to my beloved,
But my beloved had turned away and had gone!
My heart went out to him as he spoke.
I searched for him, but I did not find him;
I called him, but he did not answer me."
(Song of Solomon 5:2-6, NAS)

When there are problems of an emotional or spiritual nature, the whole sexual experience, which God gave to a husband and wife that they might be bonded together in love, may not only be reduced to nothing, but it may actually have a rupturing effect as the body goes through motions which the heart and spirit cannot tolerate. In this event a woman may receive a man physically through the front door, but lock the screen door emotionally and spiritually so that she feels nothing.

If this should happen, do not turn from the gift. Rather turn to God, the Giver, and gather healing from Him no matter what the cost. For Eros, as powerful as it may be, is fragile if not nestled in Agape love—even as the diamond you wear could never be balanced on your finger all day long were it not fastened in a setting.

You may become, with God's help, the kind of love artist you desire to become. But that desire will need to be coupled with a great deal of godliness, patience, determination, and forebearance. Some don't care to paint. Some spend their lives painting by number—afraid to choose their own colors and boundaries. Still others aspire to be a Rembrandt!

Look to your heavenly Father and watch for the stars to shine. Your night skies will be different. Some nights you will see the Milky Way and Pleiades and Orion. Other nights you will be satisfied with the North Star. Still others, against your wishes, may be completely clouded over.

Be content with what the night offers. For to grow overly concerned with the stars and their constellations is to miss the main event—the joy of the presence of the "golden moon," your beloved, and the unique privilege that is yours of growing with him in the Lord, or, if he is not a Christian, of inspiring him by your own personal growth and love to acknowledge the Giver of all of the blessings that lie at his feet.

---

[1]the *Cincinnati Enquirer,* Thursday, August 12, 1982, Section D, p. 9.

[2]Andrew Dib Sherfan, *Kahlil Gibran: The Nature of Love* (New York: Philosophical Library, 1971), p. 40.

Part Three

Be Courageous

Exercise Courage to

Begin

The wicked flee when no one is pursuing,
But the righteous are bold as a lion.
(Proverbs 28:1, NAS)

"What makes you a coward?" asked Dorothy, looking at the great beast in wonder, for he was as big as a small horse.

"It's a mystery," replied the Lion. "I suppose I was born that way. All the other animals in the forest naturally expect me to be brave, for the Lion is everywhere thought to be the King of Beasts. I learned that if I roared very loudly every living thing was frightened and got out of my way. Whenever I've met a man I've been awfully scared; but I just roared at him, and he has always run away as fast as he could go. If the elephants and the tigers and the bears had ever tried to fight me, I should have run myself—I'm such a coward; but just as soon as they hear me roar they all try to get away from me, and of course I let them go."

"But that isn't right. The King of Beasts shouldn't be a coward," said the Scarecrow.

"I know it," returned the Lion, wiping a tear from his eye with the tip of his tail; "it is my great sorrow, and makes my life very unhappy. But whenever there is danger my heart begins to beat fast...."

"Do you think Oz could give me courage?" asked the cowardly Lion.

"Just as easily as he could give me brains," said the Scarecrow.

109

"Or give me a heart," said the Tin Woodman.

"Or send me back to Kansas," said Dorothy.

"Then, if you don't mind, I'll go with you," said the Lion, "for my life is simply unbearable without a bit of courage."

"You will be very welcome," answered Dorothy, "for you will help to keep away the other wild beasts. It seems to me they must be more cowardly than you are if they allow you to scare them so easily."

"They really are," said the Lion; "but that doesn't make me any braver, and as long as I know myself to be a coward I shall be unhappy."

So once more the little company set off upon the journey.

* * * * *

"They that wait upon the Lord shall renew their strength;
they shall mount up with wings as eagles."

(Isaiah 40:31a)

I had wanted to be a missionary since a young girl, and I had yielded my life to the Lord for His direction. LaVerne and I were confident that the Lord wanted us in Burma. Yet it took courage to begin this labor. A letter, written to my parents shortly after I arrived on the mission field in north Burma, reveals some of the adventures and adjustments we experienced as we began our service:

Number 51
November 24, 1955

Dearest Mother and Dad,

How wonderful it would be just to be able to drop in and visit with you for a while, especially during this time of the year! Tomorrow is Thanksgiving Day back home, isn't it? I remember the joys of former Thanksgivings and can almost taste the luscious meals we used to have together. At least we can be with you all in spirit, and I rather think that you will be with us in spirit also. I think you would enjoy visiting us in our bamboo and grass home. We might not have a fat turkey to serve to you, but I think you would find our food quite tasty and satisfying.

For various reasons, we were not able to complete our plans for living in the vacant house across the river on the south side of Muladi Village, so we are living temporarily with the folks (Mother and Daddy Morse) in northern Muladi. Drema Esther lives in this home also. We have a bedroom, a study, and part of another room in which we can store our supplies. Eugene, Helen, and family live just across the yard, their home being parallel to ours. As I am sitting here in our study, I can hear the music of the Nam Lang River, which is ninety or so feet away. Then as I look out of one of the windows of the study, I can see a range of mountains towards the China border. From other positions we can see the snow-covered mountains towards India and those along the Tibetan border. God has blessed us so bountifully with the works of His hands. As you know, Muladi is situated in the plains area, so the ground is comparatively flat. We do so enjoy seeing the mountains, though.

We have spent the past week since our arrival here in Muladi trying to get settled down a bit. You can imagine what fun I had beautifying our two rooms with the pieces of plastic material with which you wrapped various articles in our Christmas package for the year 1954. By the way, we are now enjoying the contents of that package. Yummy, yummy! With the exception of one bed, one dresser, and one desk, we have had to furnish our rooms with boxes and trunks. Perhaps I should have said "partly furnish." We do have four low bamboo stools in our bedroom, and we borrowed a wooden bench to use here at our aluminum folding table, which serves as our desk. On the side of the room at which I am sitting there is a beautiful world globe which LaVerne bought for teaching purposes. Then next to the covered boxes on which it is resting is a blue portable organ, which is our pride and joy! There are two knee levers on the instrument which increase the volume and double the notes from E below middle C down. The natives were so grateful as I played hymns for them yesterday evening. Above the organ is a very beautiful picture of Christ in Gethsemane, which we bought before leaving Cincinnati. On the other side of the room there is a huge wall map, which LaVerne also bought for teaching purposes. While we were in Myitkyina, we ordered four chairs, a dining-room table, a kitchen cabinet, two book cases, a dresser, and two desks to furnish our home when we have one of our own. A Chinese carpenter there is making these things for us. Our beds will be made of

111

hard woven bamboo mat on top of which we will put our air mattresses. It will be fun to fix up a home of our very own. For supper this evening we had rice, beans, dried bamboo sprout soup, fat pork which LaVerne received last night after performing a wedding ceremony, tea, and the last pieces of a devil's food cake. Aside from some supplementary foods which we brought to the field with us and which we open sparingly, our diet consists mainly of rice, milk, eggs, beans, squash, bananas, papayas, one slice of bread a day, a chicken once a week, pork when it is available, and whatever meat may come in after a hunting expedition. Last night we had hornbill for supper, and it really was tasty. A couple of times we've had duck meat. Wouldn't it be wonderful if someone killed a deer? Once in a great while there may be beef available. Helen mentioned that they had had beef just shortly before we arrived as the cows, or rather, one cow of an elder here in Muladi fell off of a bridge and had to be shot.

I went down to 110 in weight, but now I believe I'm up to 111 or 112. I asked LaVerne if I could have some cans of Sweetened Condensed Milk for Christmas, and that really would be some gift as one can runs fifty cents in U. S. currency! I love the milk, and by eating it I could get fattened up a bit.

At present Mother and Eugene are in the midst of a Preachers' Convention at Robert and Betty's base in Dukdang. It's about a forty-minute ride by bicycle from Muladi. LaVerne may be going over tomorrow. Just now he is in the living room talking with some of the Christians. One of them is a native who is preaching in one of the difficult areas of the field where opium addiction is strong among the non-Christians. LaVerne and I were happy to be able to bring to the field with us some medicine for curing opium addicts which we had secured in Myitkyina through the American Baptist Mission.

As for plans for the future—LaVerne and probably Eugene will be making a trip to Tiliwago for the Christmas Convention in that area of the field and for giving further instruction and encouragement to the churches of the area. Plans are still rather unsettled, but I thought you might like to know briefly what we are hoping to do. As of present, LaVerne will be leaving on the 26th of December after the close of the Christmas Convention here, and I sincerely hope to see him again by the first of March. I am so very thankful for tiny Marcia's presence!!

Our little girl is eleven pounds plus now. She's a very healthy-looking daughter and has beautiful rosy cheeks. She's so sweet and growing prettier ever day. For some time she has been very observant of the things which are going on about her. She cries much less than she used to and spends many happy moments just lying in bed and playing with her hands. I wish so much that we had some toys for her to play with. She has only two rubber teething rings and two tiny rattles to her name. Maybe some day she'll have a few more toys. She's so very, very dear; and we do love her so. Every evening before supper Marcia and I go for a walk together around the house and down to the river. She'll be a wonderful comfort to Mommie when Daddy is gone on preaching trips.

I wasn't expecting it to be quite so cold up here, and I'm afraid we didn't adequately prepare Marcia's wardrobe for such weather. And it will be much, much colder up in the mountains at Tiliwago, where we are thinking of settling down in the future. You can imagine how thankful I was when Betty sent over some warm knitted clothing for Marcia. Back home we think we are having nice, warm weather when it's fifty or sixty degrees. That's because we have heated houses in which to live. Believe me, these bamboo houses are anything but airtight!! And when it's fifty degrees—it's COLD. When we will have freezing weather outside, we'll pretty well have the same kind of weather inside. SO—we're going to have to have some warm clothes for our little girl. I was wondering, Mother, if you could help us buy some clothes for her second year. Our layette, as you know, will only carry her through her first year. If long stockings, training pants, overalls, a snowsuit, etc., could be bought for her soon after you receive this letter, we might be able to have it here on the field before the air service stops around June or so....

Now let me plunge into an account of our journey from Myitkyina to the field, It was on the thirty-first of October that we boarded the jeep, which would take us to the beautiful village of Sumprabum. Our ride was a relatively smooth one until mile fifty-three (as reckoned from Myitkyina). At this point we left the Mali Hka River, one of the two main branches of the Irrawaddy, and I really felt as though I were travelling into the wilds. I remember the thick vegetation, the cool, refreshing streams, the beautiful sunsets, the huge, golden moon, etc. I must admit that during the close of the second day's journey, subconsciously I began to weigh the advantages and disadvantages between riding to Sumprabum on a jeep and riding on one of those horses that goes up and down on the Merry-Go-Round for several hours at a stretch. I even went into the financial angle of the matter, but I won't burden you now with such frivolous thoughts! As evening began to fall, the clouds were lined with silver— a most beautiful sight to behold. I gazed at the tremendous mountain ranges in the distance and thought of that beautiful chorus: 'Got any rivers you think are uncrossable, Got any mountains you can't tunnel through, God specializes in things thought impossible, He does the things others cannot do.' I told LaVerne that that chorus was even more meaningful when one saw mountains such as we were seeing to tunnel through. And I realized that the forces of Satan were still more impregnable. Thank God for the strength which He gives unto us as we battle through this life, ever looking forward to that time when we shall be with Him in glory. On and on we drove up the mountains towards the village of Sumprabum, which lay 4,000 feet above sea level. The sky turned a beautiful pink, and one single silver star adorned her delicate cloak. We reached the dak bungalow, a government stage house, after dark; and my, was it ever a welcome sight. As I drifted off to sleep that night in my bedroll, I remember that I thanked the Lord for the four walls that helped to keep out the cold and for the nice, warm bed with which I was blessed.

We had some difficulty while in Sumprabum trying to obtain carriers for our supplies or horses that could take our loads to the field. We managed to get five carriers to go with us (all of our tribal carriers were fellow Christians); and by Sunday, November 6, we thought things were arranged for nine horses to accompany us on our journey. On the following morning, however, the day on which we had planned to leave for the field, we had difficulty with the Chinese horsemen and finally ended up arranging for seven other horses to go in place of the nine horses on which we had first depended. The owners of the second group of horses planned

114

Lois Morse, with baby Marcia in crib on porter's back, starting their seven-day journey through jungles of Burma.

to start out on Tuesday and to catch up with us by Thursday evening. They did not agree to carry our loads on any farther, so we thought we could obtain carriers to take the horse loads on to the field. It was cloudy and misty as we began our journey approximately 1:30 P.M. on the seventh of November. I rode on a horse which we were able to arrange for me for the trip. I don't suppose I walked a mile of the way during the entire journey from Sumprabum to Muladi. (That's really something when you consider how frightened I was to ride on the ponies which we used to have on the grounds at church on Memorial Day!!) The light drizzle had turned into rain by evening time, and the path was becoming dark and slippery. I was so thankful for the horse on which I could ride and for Barnabas, our helper, who led the horse along the muddy trail with the help of a flashlight. LaVerne had given his flashlight to the boy who was carrying Marcia (she was in a specially-designed screened-in crib), so he stumbled along behind the horse, trying to follow its dark form. There wasn't a sign of a star or moon in the comfortless sky. I began to feel very, very weary in body and spirit. We hadn't been able to eat lunch because of the trouble we had with the horsemen, and I felt exceedingly empty. You can imagine how sore I felt, this being my first day on the horse. In short terms, I wasn't seasoned for the journey as yet. I sat in the saddle and wept for a long time as we journeyed slowly down the trail. We weren't sure just where the dak bungalow was or how much longer we would have to travel on in the darkness. In time we came to a section of the trail over which a huge tree had fallen; so I dismounted, and LaVerne helped me over the path. Then he and Barnabas led the horse over the difficult place. I held on to LaVerne and walked on with him for a little while.... The road was difficult, so I mounted the horse again; and onward we went. Around eight o'clock we saw the bungalow. I never saw a more welcome sight in my life! Barnabas and some of the carriers went to begin cooking the rice while others went with LaVerne to meet the other carriers who had not yet come....

I awakened on the morrow feeling much better after a good night's rest and a full stomach! It was another rainy day in which to travel. I remember that as we began our journey in the morning I looked at my wedding ring as my hand

Lois attending baby Marcia on the trail to Muladi Village, Kachin State, Burma. Note the specially designed screened-in crib to keep out malarial mosquitoes and blood-sucking leeches.

rested on the horn of the saddle and thought of the pledge of Ruth which had been sung at our wedding—'Entreat me not to leave thee, and to return from following after thee; for whither thou goest, I will go; and where thou lodgest, I will lodge; thy people shall be my people, and thy God my God; where thou diest, will I die, and there will I be buried; Jehovah do so to me, and more also, if aught but death part thee and me.' I walked a short distance that day in the rain, and my shoes became exceedingly muddy. I was beginning to wonder just how I would get them clean again, but the solution soon presented itself. The bridge was broken at the next river crossing! I was on the horse, of course, as I crossed the river; and you should have seen the beautiful shoeshine I received—and all for free! We were faced with a problem that evening as four of our carriers from Sumprabum were returning to their homes. We knew that three of them would be going only two days' journey with us; but the fourth carrier, the one who was planning to carry the baby all of the way, became terrifically ill. We sent word to a Rawang village about two miles to the north concerning our need, and you can imagine our delight when six carriers appeared on the scene in the morning. We had, besides these carriers, two boys who had reached us from the field, having been sent down by the folks, the very day we left Sumprabum.

On Wednesday, November 9, we were really having the rain! We sang hymns together as we journeyed along the trail that morning. The rain-laden jungle grass hung heavily over the leech-infested trail, and I had to spend a good deal of time trying to duck beneath the growth. You should have seen our party! The umbrellas, the horse's mane, my poncho—everything was covered with the sharp, pointed grass seeds. Sometimes I didn't manage to duck sufficiently under the jungle grass, and boy did I ever get some beautiful wet smacks in the face!! We took off the leeches which had gotten on to us during the day as we arrived at the dak bungalow that afternoon and hastened into some dry clothes. As we traveled during those three cold, rainy days, it was wonderful to realize that there would be a four-walled shelter and dry clothes at the end of our journey. Praise God from whom all blessings flow!!

On Thursday, November 10, the rain broke; and we actually saw sunlight on our trail. By mid-morning the trail was

Lois, with pony, on suspension bridge amidst monsoon jungles of Burma.

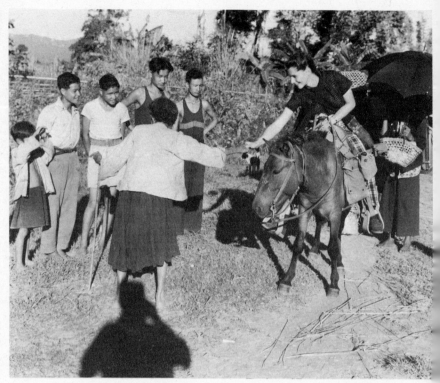
Native Christians welcoming Lois as she arrives at village in Burma.

blazing hot. As we traveled along, I suddenly heard a noise in the jungle to my left and immediately called the horse to a stop. In a moment I was staring right into the face of a black gibbon. He stared back at me, performed a bit, and then disappeared from sight. Onward we journeyed. The scarlet flowers were beautiful among the green, jungle growth; and the elephant-ear plants looked like velvet in the warm sunlight. I thrilled as I saw a pure white butterfly fluttering against the lovely, blue sky. Soon after noon we came to the bridge which stood high above a river dividing the Sumprabum Subdivision from the Putao Subdivision. As I looked at the broken bamboo sides of the bridge and gazed at the turbulent waters far below, I must admit I uttered aloud as I began to cross on my horse, 'Oh Lord, make it hold!' Well, the horse took me about a third of the way across; and then he stopped. I did all in my power to make him go ahead, but he refused to carry me any further. So we turned around and went back. I dismounted, walked across the bridge by myself, and when I had reached the other side, the horse came leisurely across. In a matter of minutes we had reached the next stage house. We had to wait here for our horse loads, so I began to boil the diapers that had collected since we had begun our trip. You should have seen the long line of baby clothes waving in the warm sunlight! It was really a sight to behold—especially for the natives!

The horses didn't catch up with us on Thursday evening as we had planned. We figured that they had had trouble because of the unexpected rains. During the day we looked eagerly towards the bridge which we had crossed the day before, looking for a sign of the horses carrying our loads. By supper time they still hadn't come, so we decided to go on ahead without them and leave a note for the preacher who was accompanying the party of horses and two Chinese horsemen. The carriers needed to return as quickly as possible to their homes to harvest their fields, and we couldn't make them wait any longer. Incidentally, one of them did go on home to his field; so there was one less man in our party. Well, about five minutes after we had made this decision, we saw the horses coming across the bridge dividing the Sumprabum and Putao Subdivisions. What a joyous sight, and how thrilled we were when the horsemen finally agreed to carry our loads on to within one day's journey of the field.

As we began our journey the next day, we passed thousands and thousands of spider webs which lay by the roadside. The dew which covered them glistened in the sunlight. I wish you could have seen the exquisite butterflies which we watched as we journeyed on the overland trip. I never dreamed that such beautiful creatures existed. The next time we make such a journey we should by all means take a butterfly net with us. I can imagine that Marcia will have a lot of fun catching and collecting butterflies from this part of the world. I want to get a good book on butterflies when we do go home. We continued down the trail; and as I rode on the horse, I began to sing that glorious song of hope, 'When I Shall Come to the End of My Way.' Even as I sang, LaVerne, who was following behind me, called to my attention the

Tibetan borderland mountains, which could be seen in the distance. Shortly after we had passed some wild elephant tracks, we saw the welcome sign, 'Inspection Bungalow,' which meant our day's journey was ended.

November 13 was the Lord's Day, so we didn't travel on that day. Services were held with the carriers in the morning, afternoon, and evening. How we did thank the Lord for His watchful care over us all along the way.

The next morning I roused and gave the baby her 6:00 A.M. feeding.... Soon the carriers were ready to go with their approximate sixty-pound loads, and we followed shortly after them. It was fun to listen to the gibbons playing in the early morning sunlight. As we continued on with our journey, I began to feel quite blue about living such an unsettled life for so many months—with no prospects of being able to settle down in our own home for some months to come.... Well, I began to feel so blue that I realized that it was time to give myself another mental spanking. My first thoughts were those of Paul and of the terrifically unsettled life which he led. Yet, he was completely happy for he had learned how to be happy in the Lord. My conclusion: "There is absolutely no basis for feeling dejected because your life may be one of continual upsets, etc. Lord, help me to grow in Thee." The turmoil which possessed my mind continued to be with me for about an hour or so. In fact, I was so engrossed in my thoughts that I hardly knew what was going on about me. I was jolted back to reality when I heard someone giving me instructions to dismount as an elephant was coming down the road. I did so gladly. We all hastened into the brush on the side of the road to make plenty of room for the huge animal to pass. On top of the elephant was a native with his load of goods. I mounted my horse again and soon brought my thoughts to a conclusion. They may be summed up thusly: There is a terrific difference between being happy "in the Lord" and being happy "in the blessings of the Lord." Perhaps many times we believe we know what it means to be happy in the Lord when really we are leaning heavily for our happiness upon momentary blessings which happen to be ours. I speak for none other but myself. The real test comes when some of these momentary blessings are knocked out from under us. We should be truly happy no matter what the outward circumstances may be if we have grown enough to know what it means to be happy in Him. I suppose that's a lifelong process.

In the early afternoon we came to the worst stage house which I had ever laid eyes on in my youthful experiences. It was a filthy, mainly one-roomed affair. As I fed Marcia her vitamins and juice . . . I gazed at the holes in the grass roof and through the holes of the floor to the animals which wandered about underneath. There was a newer stage house a bit farther along the trail, but it was decided that we should remain here as it was much nearer to the congregation to which LaVerne was supposed to speak in the evening. There was a tiny room to the side of the main room, which we soon converted into a bedroom for Marcia and me. I calmly watched LaVerne as he pushed the dirt through the holes of the floor with a poor excuse of a broom and smilingly re-marked, "This is what it means to be happy in the Lord!" He also smiled, recalling the discussion of the morning. As he blew up the air mattress for my bed, I said, "It surely does take a lot of air to blow up those things." He simply replied, "Yes, they were made for preachers!"

The following morning we stood without the stage house with some natives of the village and our helper, Barnabas, and prayed, as was our custom, before undertaking the jour-ney of the day. A million or more gnats hovered about us. Tears came to my eyes as I thanked the Lord for giving us life and health and strength to see this day. This was the last day of our journey to the field. We traveled on and on, ea-gerly watching the sign posts along the way. By late after-noon we reached the village of Muladi on the edge of the plains. The Christians left their work in the fields along the road to come out and greet us. Others hurried from their houses to our path. I had to choke back the tears as I noticed one little girl who all but pushed everyone out of her way on the porch of her home so she could get down the steps first to greet us. Well, it was a wonderful, wonderful day; and we thanked the Lord for His blessings. As we neared the home of the folks, I dismounted and planned to go ahead of the party to surprise them all. But soon we saw Eugene coming down the road toward us on his motor bike. We greeted him happily, and then I rushed on to the folks' home. Mother and Helen saw me as I neared the porch of the home. You can imagine how anxious we were to uncover tiny Marcia and show her off to all of the folks, including her little boy cousins. Daddy was in the fields, so he didn't know of our arrival until some time later. It was good to see Drema Esther again. I wish you could know her. I know you would love her even as the rest of us do. She's one exceptional girl.

On Saturday evening after the service at the church, Mother or Daddy mentioned to me as they came through the kitchen house where I was boiling bottles that it had been announced that I would speak on the morrow. I used as a topic for my devotional thoughts, "The Adoption of Sons," using as a text the latter part of the seventh verse of the twenty-first chapter of Revelation. In beginning I pointed out the reason for man's existence upon the earth as is seen in the fact that man alone, out of all of God's creation, was made with a capacity for fellowship with God. I continued with these thoughts for a short while and then discussed the question, "Who is like unto our God?" I then closed with an exhortation to be grateful unto the Father for His bountiful blessings.

Daddy just walked in and said to give you his love and heartiest greetings. Soon he, LaVerne, and I will be heading on our bicycles for Dukdang to attend part of the Convention.

Monday was an eventful day for all of us here. I was busy in the kitchen with Esther when suddenly she cried, "Airplane!!" We all rushed out to see this silver bird from civilization. We felt as though we were in touch with the outside world again. It was a test flight, and word was given that the flights would be coming in once a week. Ah, now perhaps we can get our supplies up to the field before too many more months pass by. Many of Helen's and Gene's things have to be flown up also. And we're all running very, very short of flour and sugar, which must be flown to us from Myitkyina unless there is a dependable escort who could accompany the supplies overland. Oil for cooking also must be flown to the field as the only oil available here for cooking tastes like cod liver oil! ...

There are no doubt a thousand and one things which I wanted to tell you in this letter, but I must bring this letter to a close.

Thank you for all of your prayers for us. God has been so good to us. Especially do we thank Him continually for the most priceless bundle which He has given to us. Marcia is so very dear and such a beautiful child. It's so much fun to talk with her and love her and to see her smile and coo at us. I hasten to bring this to a close. God keep you all—and by the time you receive this I expect Christmas greetings will be in order. God be praised for His only Son, for in Him, and in Him alone, there is hope.

All of our love, with prayers, and thanksgiving
for our loved ones back home—
Lois, LaVerne, and Marcia

Exercise Courage to

Remain

They shall run, and not be weary.
(Isaiah 40:31)

Many times we faced joys and sorrows in our years of service in Burma. It took courage to remain there. Letters were written frequently to our supporters to share with them our progress and to petition their prayers. The following letter is one that I wrote to the church that supported me while we were in Burma. It tells of some of the difficulties I faced and some of the joys I experienced.

Dukdang Village
January 30, 1957

Our very dear Friends and Co-laborers in Christ:

Greetings in the name of our precious Lord and Savior, Jesus Christ! Isn't it wonderful to be a Christian? Isn't it wonderful to know that this life, with all of its temptations, heartaches, frustrations, and failures is but a shadow that will swiftly pass to a life of glorious bliss and joy unspeakable? Even the greatest joys of our earthly days will seem so infinitely, so immeasurably small on that wondrous day when the clouds shall no longer hide the glory of His face. Until then, may His richest blessings rest upon you all; and may you each one be given sufficient daily strength to accomplish with joy those things which He has called you to do

127

for the glorification of His name. How well I love the thought of that poem, "Strength for today is all we need, For there never will be a tomorrow; For tomorrow will prove but another today With its measure of joy and sorrow."

It is afternoon now as I am writing this letter to you. Marcia is sleeping in her crib beneath some nice, warm blankets in the bedroom on the other side of the house. It is very cold this time of year, though the temperature rarely falls below 40°; but that still is quite cold considering the "warmth" of these bamboo and grass houses in which we live. Our only heat at nighttime is a hot-water bottle and a pile of warm blankets, and in the early mornings and evenings we can huddle about the fireplace in the center of the front room. In the meantime, though, the cold wind comes sweeping in through the myriads of holes in the woven bamboo mats which form the floors and walls of our house, and likewise through the huge openings in the roof connections. I must admit, however, that either this winter's weather or Lois has changed considerably since the previous cold season for I do not notice the biting cold nearly so much this year as I did last year. I rather believe that the change has occurred in the latter rather than in the former, which simply proves that individuals possess a surprising capacity for toughening when they find themselves without the comforts they once knew!

One thing that we do enjoy about the cold weather is the fact that there is usually plenty of fresh pork available. In the past several weeks we've all been busy rubbing fire-hot salt into pieces of meat and hanging them over our fireplaces to smoke for use throughout the present year for flavoring rice and available vegetables. Mother, Daddy, and Esther killed the pig they had been fattening; but Eugene and Helen, not having one, bought meat from the Lisu in their village. . . . We also had been buying our meat from the villagers as our pig was not sufficiently fattened to kill this winter. Nonetheless—-about 2:30 on the morning of the third, I heard our pig in its pen just a few feet from our house give a terrifying squeal, which nerve-shaking noise was accompanied by the shouting of our two Rawang girl helpers in the back room of the house! LaVerne hastened with our .22 Hornet rifle to the pigpen along with the two girls only to find that our prospective pork chops, hams, and the like had disappeared into the blackness of the night. Near the pen was a huge tiger track, and there was a wide swath through the tall grass leading to the jungle where the huge animal had evidently charged through. They searched the yard and adjoining fields by the light of our Coleman lantern but could find no trace of the pig and so, disheartened, returned to the house to get some sleep before dawn. The next morning one of the girls called excitedly to us from the path which led to the well. There, a few feet from the pen, lay the pig, decidedly dead, stiff, and cold! The tiger had bitten clear trough its skull into the brain but had evidently been frightened in the process of carrying away its victim by the sound of the Hornet. You can imagine how thankful we were to God, especially when we found that the blood had drained properly! I vowed that I would take Marcia on a picnic the day our pig was killed, scraped, and dismembered; but to my great amazement, I found myself working right along with the others.

Rice forms the main bulk of our diet. We eat rice porridge for breakfast, fried rice with bits of egg, onion, and meat for lunch, and boiled rice with accompanying dishes for supper. Recently, we have been able to obtain some marble-sized potatoes; and they really afford a most welcome change. We usually have bananas and papayas in the fruit line, but there are practically no vegetables available except greens. Last year we were able to buy some cabbages from the Shan women, but it doesn't seem as though there will be any this year.

Marcia is adjusting very well to her home here in Dukdang and is quickly learning the art of living in this part of the world. In the early evenings our two helpers are busy cutting firewood in the back of the yard for the fireplace in the front room and the wood-burning stove. One day Marcia decided to help Ayin, one of the girls, to carry the wood into the kitchen. Accordingly, she marched ahead of her, hugging two pieces of firewood close to herself, put them down on the woven bamboo floor in the kitchen, tried to open the door of the stove, and finally succeeded in doing so with a little help from Mother. Then she promptly placed the wood into the stove and put her little face as close as possible to the tiny door opening and blew several times to get the fire started!! Guess who was beaming with pride and joy??

Day by day the gospel continues to spread in this part of

God's earth, which is no more distant from His dwelling place than our own beloved homeland. Souls are continually born into the Kingdom, and those already within the fold are drawn nearer to their Savior through the faithful ministries of His Lisu and Rawang servants.

Our hearts have been thrilled recently with the incredible registration of 435 students, of both the Lisu and Rawang tribes, for the present six-week Bible school being held in Muladi Village by Mother, LaVerne, and Eugene, with two of the Rawang leaders, Peter and Tychicus, also teaching and translating. This massive student body consists largely of men and women who have been selected by the elders of their respective churches throughout the mission field. Some have come from as far as fifteen days' journey away that they might gather with others to learn more of His Word. Classes run from 8:00 to 1:00 in the morning and then again from 2:00 to 4:00 in the afternoon; conferences are held until late in the night to discuss church and evangelistic problems with various ministers present. We know that you will rejoice with us in this work and unite your praise and thanksgiving with ours for the eagerness of these people to know more of His holy Word. Be praying continually for those teaching that they might receive sufficient daily strength for this tremendous task at hand.... We do pray that each individual student might be drawn closer to his Lord during this time.

We do want to thank you for the letters which we have received in the past months.... Please be praying fervently that we might be able to keep in better touch with our loved ones back home. So much of our mail has gotten lost in the past months since August of last year, and the burden has been heavy upon our hearts....

We remember you unceasingly in our prayers and trust that you are growing in number and spirit and serving Him with joy, bearing your daily crosses with a song upon your lips because of the blessed hope which is set before you.

Yours in Christ,
Lois, LaVerne, and Marcia

Exercise Courage to

Begin Anew

They shall walk, and not faint.
(Isaiah 40:31)

On Sunday, January 25, 1981, the 444-day-old nightmare was finally over. The fifty-two American hostages held in Iran were safely aboard a jetliner--homeward bound. As I sat in front of my television and watched them departing from Germany—waving their goodbyes as the band played on—tears flowed. But they were flowing for something more than the hostages' release. I was experiencing one of those quiet moments of inner awareness which comes to us when we discover reservoirs of emotion which, unknown to us, still lie in the depths of our beings.

Now, in these moments of private recall, I stand at attention and salute with love and esteem all of the willing hostages who have gone forth from this country, not necessarily following their own natural inclinations, but constrained by the love of Christ, to carry the gospel to a dying world. Hundreds and thousands have gone into every corner of the globe—some to stay, some to return home. As was true in the case of the Iranian hostages, each is a unique individual, responding to life in a unique way, coming back home with a unique story to tell.

Some who went forth remained in the company of those who spoke their own language and thus were able to retain intimate companionship with fellow humans. Others were placed in "solitary confinement," language-wise, not even knowing how to make the simplest intelligible sounds nor how to understand anyone around them. Some were able to escape from this confinement quickly, taking advantage of trained personnel and applying themselves rigorously to the task. Others, struggling with meager assistance and little aptitude for learning a foreign language, suffered extreme isolation. Some, emotionally mature and in a field that satisfied their deepest personal needs, were able to go forth with joy and reach their maximum fulfillment in spreading the gospel of Christ. Others, emotionally immature and in a field that aggravated their deepest needs, withdrew and were relatively impotent to spread the gospel.

When furlough time came, some were happy to be returning home. Others were so depressed they couldn't enter into the festivities planned. Some were bitter. Others were not. Some were relatively healed from their long ordeal. Others would live for years with memories that would have as tenacious a hold on them as the Iranian captors had over the hostages. Some were able to meet the high demands of the public. Others were not.

Unlike the fifty-two hostages returning from Iran, only some received the individualized attention they needed. Others were neglected. "You failed! You need help, brother! No cheers for you!" And I gather these in my embrace and break down and weep.

Not all stories are exactly as they seem. My own years on the Tibetan border seemed to me, in many ways, like a time of solitary confinement. Surrounded by tens of thousands, I was alone. For years I tried valiantly to break through the walls that closed me in. I struggled with the language. I struggled with the primitive setting. I struggled with the culture. I struggled, bereft of things and people held too dear. I struggled with myself. Years passed. Problem piled upon problem. The billows and waves rolled over me until I hung onto the railing of life, as one seasick and tempest tossed. The heaving over, part of me would weep for the girl who once was—the high-school girl who wanted above all else to devote her life to missionary work. Yet, in some strange way, part of me knew, as no one else could, that the girl who stood there with faintly burning wick was really stronger and closer to God's intentions for the building of character than

132

the young girl who stood so outwardly buoyant with flame held high over twenty-five years ago.

"A Roman coin was once found with the picture of an ox on it; the ox was facing two things—an altar and a plough; and the inscription read: *'Ready for either.'*" [1] Could it be that some are sent to serve, while God, in His infinite wisdom, permits others to go for the purpose of becoming? For a task yet to be fulfilled? And if this be so, does it not alter the usual standard of judgment? I advance this question not for my own sake—for it matters not to me how I may be judged in this area by any person. But I would disarm anyone who would set himself up as judge over others—especially the hurting and the unsure.

Standing alone at the window of my room in the Thamada Hotel, downtown Rangoon, Burma, roughly fourteen years after leaving the field, I looked down upon the streets of the city. It was midnight. In moments words welled up within me, and I penned these lines:

"Burma—land of great joys, land of deep sorrows—I love you! I pull my curtain aside and search for you in the lighted darkness. Standing there, I find myself pulling back the curtain of my soul. I embrace you with yearnings and longings relieved only by my tears. I am at home in my heart in your presence with a wholeness that is not mine when I am absent from you.

"I have ridden your smooth tree-lined streets and hiked your jungle trails. I have birthed my babies within your boundaries and am strangely stirred for 'twas here they uttered their first mortal cries and took their first tottering steps. I have given your people the best I had to offer and only regret that my best was lacking because of my own struggles to grow and to be. Land of my pain, I have become because of you what I could never have attained apart from you for I had to struggle to win the victory with a fierceness and relentlessness that drove me onward.

"Filter every pore of my being this night and grant me peace. Sleep will not come. It matters not! There are other nights to rest. Embrace me in the darkness of this hour and rise and walk with me at daybreak's dawning."

It is true, what God has promised, "A bruised reed He will not break, And a dimly burning wick He will not extinguish" (Isaiah 42:3, NAS). Look! I am learning to balance myself as a child before he takes his first tottering steps! I am able, by

God's grace, to stand and look at you and not be over-whelmed when you chat with me about missions. Do not walk away from me. I am standing! And that is a triumph known only to those who must learn to walk again.

Willing hostages all, I salute you. But I save my deepest embrace for those men and women who have been scarred emotionally and psychologically, some beyond recognition. Some will remain in America. Others, though burdened, will return to the field—not in a B-52 as one Iranian hostage was wont to do if ever he returned to Iran, but with the love of Christ. Whatever your circumstances may be, have compassion on your dimly-burning flame. Do not despise it nor, more tragic still, allow it to make you turn and despise yourself. Christ will fan your flame again in His own time, in His own way. Until then, know you will be carried in His deepest embrace. If it were not so, what message of hope would there be to carry to the heathen?

Now, it is my fervent prayer that as all of the yellow ribbons put up in remembrance of the Iranian hostages have come down from the trees and telephone poles across the land, that we who are in Christ will tie a *red* ribbon around every tree, telephone pole, and bamboo clump in the world to remind men and women everywhere of the hostages Satan has taken. Some are heathen. Some are missionaries who, though "bound" themselves, go to free the heathen. Some are sinners. Some are saints who pass by each other with smiles on their faces and the rattle of chains around their feet. All are men and women who, for one reason and another, have not yet found the freedom that God intends and yearns for them to have.

Let us work tirelessly and pray unceasingly for one another's release—hugging each other, crying on each other's shoulders for joy when the job is completed—all in the name of Christ. Beautiful Savior! Blessed Redeemer!

---

[1]William Barclay, *The Gospel of Matthew* (Philadelphia, Pennsylvania: The Westminster Press, 1957, 1958), II, p. 254-255.

Exercise Courage to

Parent

A rose in full bloom and a little rosebud shared the same stem, the same rain, and the same sunshine. But one was close to beginning, and the other close to ending.

The little rosebud looked at the rose in full bloom with envy and awe. Her opened petals, laden with raindrops, shimmered in the sunlight. "What is it like to be so beautiful?" the little rosebud questioned within herself. "I am so closed in," she lamented, "so bound up I do not even know how many petals I have or if they would be beautiful if unfolded. I wonder when that day will ever come. Or will it come for me?" She dropped her eyes from the rose above her, tears mingling with the raindrops on her leaves.

Day after day went by. The rose in full bloom and the little rosebud continued to share the same stem, the same rain and the same sunshine. But one was close to beginning, and the other close to ending.

The rose in full bloom looked at the little rosebud with envy and awe. "What is it like," she questioned within herself, "to be pressed tight with loveliness, to be able to look forward to joys yet unknown, to experience the titillating taste of mysteries yet to be? I am so close to dying. I wonder when the day will come. I know that it will come for me." She lifted her eyes from the little rosebud, her tears mingling with the raindrops that graced her petals and leaves.

Two roses on a stem. One in full bloom. One yet to be. Given the choice, which rose would you be?

The mysteries of life haunt every season. We all reach out

for more. The answers to life's questions dance away from our grasp and beckon us on to God, who loves roses in full bloom and little rosebuds.

God continues to plant seeds. He continues to send the rain. He continues to send the sunshine. And generation after generation the little rosebuds and the roses in full bloom keep asking questions and reaching out for more.

* * * * *

"I think the biggest thing is example," said our nineteen-year-old daughter, Shirley, one day when we were having a discussion on parenting.

Then LaVerne added, "It's frightening when you realize that what a child thinks is normal is what he sees."

One of the rewards of my inheritance from my own parents, that has stood me through tougher times than I can relate to you, is an inner spirit of steel—even though my emotional makeup has been about as strong as a wet noodle. That inner faith, which has been tested beyond measure, is still with me and has brought me through many floodwaters. If I didn't believe that God can take any life, no matter how badly scarred that life may be, and turn that person into a functioning, healthy human being—provided there be a sufficient life span for the miracle to occur—I would personally cancel all of my speaking engagements, throw away this book before it reaches the press, cease my own struggling to do and to be, and become a nobody who wouldn't be good for anybody. I know the power God can have in a life because I've seen His power working in me and transforming me into His likeness. It is the hope that comes from the reality of that power that I wish I could transmit to others.

Actually, if a mother doesn't believe that God can do much for her, it is not likely she will believe that He can do much for her children, which leaves her in a pathetic plight. Her worrying will never cease, and this spirit of restlessness and hopelessness will be transfused into her children.

I recall years ago reading a form letter which was sent out by Clyde Narramore recounting the following incident. At the top of the letter was the picture of a teen-age boy and these words in quotes, "I DON'T THINK MUCH CAN BE DONE FOR HUMAN BEINGS . . ." Then, these words: "A few

136

days ago I struck up a conversation with a young man who was standing beside me in a department store. 'Are you in college?' I asked. The fellow tossed his bangs to one side, looked up and said, 'Yeah—majoring in psychology.' Noticing my smile, he asked, 'Are you a psychologist?' After telling him I was, he said that he had recently decided to change his major from *psychology* to *interior decorating.*

"'Why?' I asked. 'Because,' he replied, pushing his hair to one side again, 'I don't think much can be done for human beings. You can only go so far with them. I figure you can do a lot more with room furnishings than you can with people.'

"As I drove home I thought to myself, 'He doesn't think much can be done for human beings because no one has done anything spectacular for him. Furthermore, he's probably never known anyone whose life has been transformed.'"[1]

Part of what our five children have become has been because of us. Part of what they have become has been in spite of us—our weaknesses, our failings, our idiosyncrasies, and our problem areas. But most important, *all* that they have been, are, and will become continues to be in the hands of their heavenly Father who will not fail to bless them and to guide them. Oh, how often, when LaVerne and I have read the Word and prayed together for every member of our family, as is our early morning custom, have I thanked God for the beautiful job of parenting *He* has done with our children. We need to continually praise God for His faithful fathering which fills in not only the cracks and crevices but the grand canyons left in our children because of our own human parenting. He not only fills in; He makes all things work together for good in every life that loves Him—including both the parent and the child.

The best guideline I know of for parenting is that given in the thirteenth chapter of 1 Corinthians: "Love is patient, love is kind, and is not jealous; love does not brag and is not arrogant, does not act unbecomingly; it does not seek its own, is not provoked, does not take into account a wrong suffered, does not rejoice in unrighteousness, but rejoices with the truth; bears all things, believes all things, hopes all things, endures all things. Love never fails" (1 Corinthians 13:4-8, NAS).

Love your child as you would want your child to love you.

Be patient with your child as you would want your child to be patient with you. Be kind to your child as you would want your child to be kind to you. Rejoice over your child's good fortunes as you would want your child to rejoice over your good fortunes. Be humble in your dealings with your child as you would want your child to be humble in his dealings with you. Be sensitive to your child as you would want your child to be sensitive to you. Be deeply courteous to your child as you would want your child to be deeply courteous to you. Seek your child's welfare even as you would be pleased to have your child seek your welfare. Don't provoke your child to wrath even as you would not want your child to provoke you to wrath. Discipline your child even as you would want God to discipline you. Encourage your child even as you would want your child to encourage you. Be proud of your child even as you would want your child to be proud of you. Forgive your child even as you would want your child to forgive you. And when your child is old enough, let him make some of his own decisions even as you enjoy the liberty God gives to you in making some of life's decisions. Recognize and praise your child's uniqueness even as you would want your child to recognize and praise your uniqueness. Let your child stand apart from you as a separate human being—uniquely designed by God and existing for the purpose of glorifying God even as you would want to stand apart from your child as a separate human being—uniquely designed by God and existing for the purpose of glorifying God.

How often do I think of the contrast between the thoughts that Noah's father had concerning his son, and the thoughts God had for Noah. After Noah's birth, his father said, "This one shall give us rest from our work and from the toil of our hands arising from the ground which the Lord has cursed" (Genesis 5:29, NAS). And while Lamech rejoiced over his son's birth and anticipated the blessing he would be in the fields, God looked down upon the earth and "blotted out every living thing that was upon the face of the land, from man to animals to creeping things and to birds of the sky, and they were blotted out from the earth; and only Noah was left, together with those that were with him in the ark" (Genesis 7:23, NAS). Noah was singled out by God to be the one through whose family the entire human race would be preserved. God's dreams for our children are always bigger than our dreams for them could ever possibly be.

Two basic needs of children that we need to respond to as parents are

1. the need to be touched in love;
2. the need to be inspired by example.

In his book, *How to Parent,* Dr. Fitzhugh Dodson refers to a study conducted by Dr. Harry Harlow in which baby rhesus monkeys were raised by terry-cloth dummies that had built-in nursing bottles. Dr. Harlow's study revealed, "Although these monkeys received adequate nourishment, they did not get adequate amounts of contact comfort, since there were no monkey mothers around to cuddle them and give other physical demonstrations of affection. The results of the experiment showed that these baby monkeys grew up to be socially inadequate adult monkeys. They were unable to mate with receptive monkeys of the opposite sex, and they showed strange and weird mannerisms, much like those observed in human psychotics."[2]

One thing we have done consistently throughout the years besides hugging our children is to give them loving back-rubs at bedtime. They have devoured them over the years and still enjoy them when they are home. It can be a wonderful time of sharing.

Children also need to be inspired by our life-style.

While waiting at the hospital one day, I picked up the August 15, 1983, issue of *Newsweek* and turned to an article entitled, "Teen-age Suicide in the Sun Belt." In closing, it said, "As psychiatrist Mary Giffin reports in 'A Cry for Help,' coauthored with Carol Felsenthal, 'Over and over, the (suicidal) adolescents we talked to groped for words to describe what they felt was a void in their lives—the lack of anything to stand for, of an altruistic goal.' For all its enlightened attention, there is still something cruelly amiss in a society that has failed to give its children such a goal, enthroning instead a danger-fraught ethos of self-fulfillment."[3]

Whether we live or whether we die, we need to pass on to our children through our example what we believe to be life's real values.

I remember back in March, 1963, when we were living in Burma, LaVerne became extremely ill. The report from the local doctor was far from encouraging. It was necessary for him to make the long trip down to Rangoon where he could have a heart X ray and a cardiogram taken. It was decided that his mother should accompany him while I remained at home with the children awaiting further word. LaVerne changed so drastically within one week's time we had no idea what lay ahead. After he and Mother boarded the plane that carried them to Rangoon, I sat down in our grass-roofed home and read the Document of Will and Testament he had left behind:

> "... (3) I will that my love and hopes for their contin-
> ued well-being and growth in Jesus Christ be given to
> the Christians of the churches of Christ in Burma, and
> to the many dear Christians in America who have
> throughout the past years sustained and worked with
> us for the spreading of the 'unsearchable riches of
> Christ.'
>
> "(4) I will that my love and devotion be given to my
> beloved wife ... and that my love and devotion also be
> given to my very dear children, Marcia Louise Morse,
> Mark Russell Morse, Cynthia Marie Morse, and our
> child yet unborn, with the hope that they will ever re-
> member my love, and that they will love and cherish
> their mother even as I would love and cherish her.
>
> "To all concerned, I will that they wholeheartedly re-
> member that 'all things work together for good to them
> that love God; to those who are the called according to
> His purpose,' and that, above all, we may rejoice trium-
> phantly in the blessed hope and assurance of life eter-
> nal with God our Father and Jesus Christ our Risen
> Savior. Russell LaVerne Morse ... March 6, 1963."

Next to example, one of the most important parts of parenting is praise. So many children feel that no matter what they do they can never, never live up to their parents' expectations. This is very defeating to children, and contributes greatly to their inability to obtain their potential. We need to praise our children, accept them for the unique individuals that they are, and express our deep belief in them.

As parents we need to face the necessary adjustments that come in our lives and in the lives of our children when they begin leaving the nests. We need to constantly encourage them to continue exercising their gifts, accepting others in love while at the same time making responsible choices, planning for the future, and standing for their convictions.

Leaving the Nest

I walked into our "little" girl's room one day and looked carefully from one thing to another. LaVerne and I had just seen her off at the airport where she and some of her friends had taken off for Florida following their high-school graduation.

I noticed on the wall by her door a silhouette of Marcia's face and alongside it these words she had copied:

"The
flower looks
up high only to
see the light.
And never
down to see
its shadow.
This is
a wisdom
man must
learn"[4]

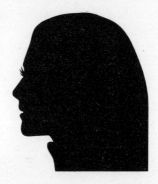

Above and to one side of the silhouette was an adorable card picturing a little tyke kneeling down writing these words: "Nobody's PERFORKT." On around the corner of her room hung a large poster with a man sitting beside the sea and this caption: "The future of the earth is in our hands. How shall we decide?" Beneath this was a composition written by one of Marcia's close friends. There were curios from different parts of the world; pop cans stacked toward the ceiling in artistic fashion; an empty tea cup with a spoon in it beside her bed—her graduation hat leaning against it from the night before; hats and pillows, etc., strewn over her bed; and a list for the graduation trip.

* * * * *

Little girl, now turned seventeen, was it only yesterday that we traveled on the trail to the Tibetan border—you in your screened-in crib and me on my horse? Remember the time (of course, you don't!) when you and I got separated on the trail? About eight o'clock that night I saw the outline of the government bungalow against the sky. Here, at last, was a place of refuge for our weary party of travelers. Barnabas and some of the carriers began to prepare the rice while Daddy and others went out into the darkness to meet those who had not yet come with their loads, including the boy who was carrying you. I sat in the dark in the front room of the wooden bungalow and prayed for your safety. Before long the rest of the party arrived. I opened the lid of your portable crib and looked at your beautiful face by candlelight. You were no less beautiful yesterday when I looked into your happy face before you marched down that aisle in your white graduation cap and gown.

My dear little girl, now grown up, we have traveled many a trail together, you and I. They've not all been by porterback and horseback; but they've been trails nonetheless. Some have led, as it were, through the meadows where the wild flowers have grown. Others have led along steep and rocky places.

Now, my daughter, there are other trails that you must climb. Your graduation cap has been worn and set aside, and you look to the life beyond. This is as it should be!

Go, find your mountain, sweetheart, and then climb it. One word of caution: Never be so eager to look at the view from the top that you lose sight of the scenery along the way. For then you will lose most of the sweetness of life.

God keep you, "little" girl, and guard your feet from stumbling or losing the way.

And as you climb, sweetheart, some day you *will* find your dream!

* * * * *

Now, Lord, I need to talk just to You. You understand that, don't You? My heart ached when she told me about it, Lord. You see, Marcia had always wanted a banana tree. Today was the day! She went to the garden center nearby, chose one, and brought it home. Oh, she was so proud of it!

It wasn't just the tree itself, Lord, that raised her to such heights. It was the fact that in transplanting the tree, she was really transplanting a part of her childhood from the borders of Tibet to suburban America.

We had so much fun trying to decide just where to plant it. I watched as she carried the plant from one spot to another. We decided it looked best by the rose arbor down by the garden. But, Lord, the winds were especially fierce that day. In their fury, they snapped the two, tall, graceful fronds of the young tree. When she told me about it, my heart sank with hers.

When her father returned home that night, he said the tree needed to be planted by the side of the house where it would be protected from the winds. I know he's right, Lord. Still, in my mind's eye, I'll always see it down by the rose arbor in the back yard; its tall fronds swaying gracefully in the breeze! Oh, Lord, it was so beautiful.

Lord, my girl is blooming into womanhood now. She's thinking seriously about her life and wondering what to do with it. One day she picks it up as a plant, places it in a spot, and asks me how it looks. Still another day she puts it somewhere else and asks me how it looks there! Lord, my wisdom is so little. Instinctively, I want her to be planted by the rose arbor, tall and beautiful, swaying in life's breezes, not knowing her as You do, Lord, nor understanding that I might be planting her where the fierce winds would snap her potential.

Please, Lord, plant my little girl for me. Help her always to reach toward the sunlight of Your love. Help her to bear fruit in its season and feed the souls of men as they travel down the road beside her. May her branches shade the children of men as they seek for rest from the burdens of the day.

And, Lord, this one last request. Please stand beside her when the fierce winds come so they won't snap her graceful spirit. But if, in Your providence, You allow it to be snapped, care for her ever so gently, Lord, till new growth appears and she is swaying beautifully in life's breezes once again!

Exercising Gifts

One of my favorite things is eating out with my kids. One day I drove downtown to be with Cindy during her lunch break. On previous occasions when we had talked together about her gifts, I had commented on the fact that everything she did, both with her hands and with her mind, she did well—which was true. However, my encouragement was so vague as to be ineffectual. This time when we visited, I shared with Cindy that I thought her real gift was the gift of giving encouragement to others and that all of the other things she did so well were simply tools the Lord had put into her hands so she could minister to the needs of others— even as a carpenter has different tools at his disposal in order to do his job effectively. Suddenly, Cindy, who in her inner frustration had thought of concentrating on one thing, saw her whole life from a different perspective. It was as though a picture window had been constructed in the wall of her mind, enabling her to look out upon her life from a different vantage point.

I recall another day when Cindy was seated in the recliner in the family room reading something I had written. She hadn't gotten far when she commented, "I know you have to do different kinds of writing, Mom, but this is your gift."

Cindy's comment opened up a whole new horizon for me. It was deeply helpful because I had noticed that whereas I was able to flow when involved with certain kinds of writing, other things I had written left me with a troubled, agitated feeling. I couldn't quite figure it all out until Cindy made the comment she did, and I realized that my gift wasn't just writing in general, but a specialized kind of writing involving indentification with the human struggle.

We really do need each other to help call forth each other's gifts.

* * * * *

Precious Cindy,

Nearly twenty-two years ago when you were as fresh in this world as the morning dew, you opened your tiny mouth and uttered your first cry. As you well know, that cry did not echo within the palace walls of a king but pierced the grass roof of a house on stilts and reached for Tibetan skies! Some might say, "A humble beginning!" Nay, 'tis not so! I tell you, yours was a royal beginning! For though you were loaned to Daddy and to me and filled our anxious, waiting arms, you were born the child of a King!

And when He made you, Cindy, since He is a King, He did not fill you with mediocre gifts to be laid aside or given little thought. For months before your birth, from the very moment of conception, He was busy filling your tiny body,

144

mind, and soul with royal gifts fit for a princess, gifts straight from His royal palace. It was His intent that all of these be not only for your joy and delight but for the joy and delight of all who would have the blessing of experiencing the touch of your life on theirs.

When you were little and received with childish delight gifts that were given by those who loved you, it never even occurred to you to be impatient with the wrapping paper and the ribbons and bows. Even so, my darling girl, be patient with God's wrappings. Learn to love the questions you cannot yet answer even while you search and pray for understanding. Let the mysteries of life always draw you close to God, not away from Him in frustration and in pain. For in Him lie all the mysteries of Heaven and of earth, and He has promised that to him who knocketh, it shall be opened unto him. Some gifts may be opened in a moment. Others may take part of a lifetime. Whatever the case, God will help you to unwrap each gift in His own time. While you open some gifts, you will be shaking others—wondering what great treasure lies inside. Be content with this.

Walk happy through life, darling. I say, "Walk," but when I think of you, I do not see you walking. I envision a light, happy spirit winging her way through life with star-filled eyes! I want it always to be that way.

Don't stumble over the ribbons!

Accepting Others, at the Same Time Making Responsible Choices

One day while leafing through my daughter Beth's poetry, I ran across this poem, written December 4, 1979, when Beth was sixteen years old. It sums up beautifully the importance of accepting others for who they are and not trying to make them into what we want them to be. It also shows the courage we need in order to exercise our responsibility in our choice of intimate companions.

> It's really not all up to me.
> It's mainly up to you!
> I've tried so hard, but still I can't
> Control the things you do.
> It's not that I don't love you, and

145

It's not that I don't care.
But watching how you hurt yourself
Is just too much to bear.
So please try to believe me
When I say it's for the best.
I care about you also,
But my heart just needs a rest!
I want to help you straighten out;
I'd do it if I could.
If you won't do it for yourself,
When do you think you would?

Planning for the Future

Upon the occasion of his graduation from high school, our son, Mark, delivered this address on the meaning of graduation.

Tonight is graduation night. But what does 'graduation' really mean? It has different meaning for each of us. It may mean a time of celebration—we're finally going to get that diploma we've been working for these past twelve years. Graduation may mean a time of relief—exams are over, although hopefully learning hasn't stopped; we can feel the warm summer coming; and we can set our spirits free. Graduation may mean a time of crying—this is a happy occasion but this may be the last time we will ever see many of our friends. Some of you parents may be crying—you're proud of your sons or daughters, and you want to see them go on and succeed, but the sons and daughters may be leaving home (many off to college, some to get married), and parents just don't like to lose their "babies."

Graduation is a time of mixed feelings and mixed emotions. It's a time when we remember the past and anticipate the future.. We look at our past accomplishments and our past failures. Our response to these accomplishments and failures influences our future. All of us have failed sometime in the past and will fail sometime in the future. When we meet these failures, we have to respond. We can give up; say, "I can't, I can't"; develop negative attitudes; and live miserable lives full of self-criticism and self-pity. Or, we can respond positively, learn lessons, encourage ourselves, build greater determination and create future accomplishments.

146

No experience, whether a success or a failure, is wasted if it becomes part of a process of learning to do better.

Thomas Edison was a man who had great failures, but responded positively and made great accomplishments. As a boy, Edison was kicked out of school because his teachers said he was too dumb to learn. But, because of encouragement from his mother, he found the inner drive to succeed. As a teenager, Edison went deaf, but even that didn't stop him from making accomplishments. In fact, while he was deaf, he invented sound-producing machines like the phonograph. Edison didn't let other people discourage him. He encouraged himself. Because Edison responded positively to bad situations, a greater future lay ahead for him and the world!

Before we look at future success, let's thank the ones who make this success possible. First, we, the senior class of 1977, thank the entire staff of Aiken Senior High School—teachers, principals, counselors, secretaries. You've give us instruction and direction. When we've needed it most, you've given us encouragement, by your words, your expressions, by a little pat on the back or a little pat where we really needed it. We thank you for all these things—for your consideration, your help, your concern.

Next, we want to thank our parents. You've used your lives to give us life. You've taken care of our needs—our needs for warmth, for food, for shelter, for love. I would hope that every graduate here tonight wishes to take care of his parents' needs as they grow older. Parents, you've made most of our decisions for us in the past; but now we've come to a place where we will have to make many of our own decisions for the future.

Let's look, now, towards the future. We need two things for a successful future. First, we need hope. When there is no hope, there is not life. We can put our hope in money, prestige, friends, luck, good times, and even ourselves. And we need money, friends, and good times; but if we put our ultimate hope in these things, we'll be hurting ourselves and our lives may become fruitless and empty. We can't depend on these things. They change! When they die, our hope in them dies; and when hope dies, we begin to die. But we must have hope—hope in something solid, hope in something that will always be, hope in something that doesn't change (even though we change), hope . . . in God.

The second need is direction. Dr. Laurence J. Peter once said, "If you don't know where you're going, you will probably end up somewhere else."[5] Each of us needs direction; each of us needs a goal. We have a common goal: to use the talents God has given us to serve mankind—not to please men, but to serve them. Our future accomplishments will be weighed not by what we have, what we are, or what we can do, but by what we do for each other with the gifts we have.

Thomas a Kempis once wrote: "For God weighs more the love out of which a man works, than the work which he does. He does much who loves much. He does much who does a thing well. He does well who serves the community rather than his own will."[6]

Each of us is special; each of us is important. Each of us has some talent, some gift, with which we can serve. Let's find that gift, cultivate it, use it to help others, and we'll succeed.

Use past experiences to help build future achievements; encourage yourself and others; and we'll graduate. Make goals; choose a pathway of life; and we'll graduate. Have hope in God; use whatever talents God gave you to serve mankind with love, and we'll graduate to a fuller, richer life, a successful future, a new day. THAT is graduation!

Standing Up for Convictions

Shirley, upon the occasion of her graduation from high school, addressed the faculty, parents, and graduates in her presidential address. Then, in her valedictory address, she delivered this challenge with her own conviction.

Life is like an important game. And each of us decides whether we sit the bench, or whether we play in that game. The future is uncertain, so playing the game involves risks. It may mean risking our pride in order to love when we might not get love in return. It may even mean putting our jobs on the line to stand up for what we think is right. Playing the game will mean working hard and enduring trials and pains. Graduates, are we willing to take the risks? Are we willing to run the race? Afraid of failure? Friends, failure in life is inevitable. But through failure we can learn how *not* to do something. On the ladder of success, we might advance three steps, and then fall back two. But still, we are farther than before, and that is what's important.

And tonight I'm not just talking about success in the outside world. I'm talking about success within ourselves . . . the development of our own character.

Bo McMillan of the Kentucky Colonels said of his team, "We do not pray to win, we pray to play." We must get involved . . . we must play the game. Because of the uncertainty of fulfilling the goals which we have established for our future, we must have courage.

First, we must have the courage to believe in ourselves. Believing in ourselves means trusting in God, having confidence in our talents and abilities, and being able to willingly use them for good. Without self-confidence, any success is improbable. In anything we do, we must enable people to have confidence in us, and we can do this when we have faith that we can meet the challenges we face in life.

Many people find inspiration and courage through poetry. On the wall of our Natatorium, members of the swim team kept a copy of a poem in which we found the inspiration to keep going even when we were exhausted:

The Man Who Thinks He Can

"If you think you are beaten, you are;
If you think you dare not, you don't;
If you'd like to win, but think you can't,
It's almost a cinch you won't.
If you think you'll lose, you're lost,
For out in the world we find
Success begins with a fellow's will;
It's all in the state of mind. . . .
Life's battles don't always go
To the stronger or faster man;
But soon or late the man who wins
Is the man who thinks he can."[7]
—Walter D. Wintle

Yes, we must have the courage to have confidence in ourselves.

And secondly, believing in ourselves gives us the courage to stand up for our convictions. In the future, we may be in a totally new environment. Our high school peers will go their own ways. At some point in time we might be alone in our beliefs of what is right and wrong. We cannot simply go along with the crowd because the crowd is always changing. We must stand firm in our convictions, no matter what the cost. We must believe in something. If you believe in God, then stand up for your conviction that what He says is right.

Martin Luther King, Jr. took a stand for his convictions. He had confidence in himself and in what he fought for. His whole life was a testament to the equality of man, which he based on his belief in God. Despite endless opposition, he had the courage to stand firm and to persevere. Believing in ourselves will give us the courage to stand up for our convictions.

Thirdly, standing up for our convictions will require the courage to endure whatever situations may arise. There's no doubt that there will be rough times when we just want to give up. Many of us will have to interview for 30 jobs before we get a chance to work. Some of us may have to settle for a job that we really don't want, or that we feel overqualified for before we find the career that's right for us. But we must push on and overcome these hardships to obtain the goals which we have set for our lives. We cannot give up.

There was a man who encountered many trials and who failed at many things. His childhood was full of hardships. Even during his manhood, the trials continued. His first candidacy for legislature was unsuccessful. His business went bankrupt and it took him 15 years to pay off his debts. Later, he failed in his first bid for Congress. Even when he was finally elected into Congress, he did not please his supporters, so he only served one term. This man had two unsuccessful bids as Senator. And in 1856 he lost a bid to become the Vice-Presidential nominee. Still, he didn't give up. Thus, in 1861, he became the sixteenth president of the United States. This man was Abraham Lincoln. He endured the hardships, he endured the struggles, he endured the pain. Because he had the courage to endure, he accomplished many things, he helped many people, and he changed the lives of everyone in this auditorium.

We can never run from the future, but we can face the

future when we have the courage to have confidence in ourselves, the courage to stand up for our convictions, and the courage to endure hardships.

We must be a part of the race of life. To win isn't the most important thing, but to have the desire to is!

Winston Churchill was asked to speak to a group graduating from Harrow School. The graduates excitedly awaited what they thought would be a long and beautiful oration. His speech speaks to all of us and summarized the underlining factor of success:

"Young gentlemen, Never, never, never,
never give up!"

* * * * *

I would like to close these few thoughts on parenting with this tribute to my children and their spouses, which hopefully every parent could also express:

> My children, as one sits and watches the sunrise and the sunset—not to seek out how God's workmanship may be improved, but to revel in the beauty and majesty of God's creation, so do I observe you.
>
> Even more! For the sun cooperates with its Maker without its will and therefore cannot have a part in enhancing its intrinsic beauty. Whereas I have seen you move at will to the rhythm of God, and as co-workers with Him in your creation, heighten your intrinsic beauty till I watch and become mute with feelings and thanksgivings too profound for words.

[1]Clyde Narramore, Narramore Christian Foundation, Rosemead, California. Used by permission.

[2]Dr. Fitzhugh Dodson, How to Parent (New York: The New American Library, Inc., 1971), p. 47.

[3]Newsweek, August 15, 1983, p. 74.

[4]Kahlil Gibran, Secrets of the Heart, (Kansas City, Missouri: Hallmark Cards, Inc., 1968), p. 55.

[5]Dr. Laurence J. Peter, The Peter Principle (New York: William Morrow & Company, Inc., 1969), p. 159.

[6]Thomas a Kempis, The Imitation of Christ (Chicago: Moody Monthly), p. 33.

[7]Poems That Live Forever, ed. Hazel Felleman (Garden City, New York: Doubleday & Company, Inc., 1965), p. 310.

The Morse Family

Front row left to right: Micah Odor, LaVerne Morse, Lois Morse, Marcia Odor, Megan Odor.

Second row left to right: Eric Morse, Jill Morse, Mark Morse, Cynthia Mizener, Dale Mizener.

Third row left to right: Shirley Morse, Kent Odor, Dale Schlensker, Beth Schlensker.

Exercise Courage to

Serve

I spent my whole life sitting in my boat mending my nets while Christ stood patiently on the sandy shore saying, "Come, follow Me."

It was incredible. He made all the flaming sunsets and the cattle on a thousand hills and every girl and boy. But He was thirsty. He had no rope. He had no bucket, and the well was deep. But He wasn't going to perform any miracle for selfish purposes! He was one of us.

Looking to one whom He had fashioned with His own hands, He asked with unequaled humility, "Give Me a drink" (John 4:7, NAS). If it were not already recorded in Scripture, it ought to be in Ripley's *Believe It or Not!*

Even so today, Christ sits by the well of every woman's life and asks for a drink. And one by one, each passes by.

One responds with false humility: "How is it that You should ask me for a drink? I am nothing." And she continues on her way, preoccupied with her person.

Another responds with false goals: "How is it that You should ask me for a drink? If I hesitate for any reason, I will never reach my journey's end." And she continues on her way, preoccupied with her position.

Still another responds with false priorities: "How is it that You should ask me for a drink? Don't You see that if You don't get up off that well You will fall in, for it is so badly in need of repair?" And she continues on her way, preoccupied with her problems.

153

Then one passes by who possesses the mind of Christ: "I do not know how it is that You should have need of me. But I have a rope. I have a bucket, and the well is deep. I shall draw for You." She preoccupies herself with Christ's thirst. And God's name is hallowed wherever she goes.

"Then the righteous will answer Him, saying, 'Lord, when did we see You hungry, and feed You, or thirsty, and give You drink?' ... And the King will answer and say to them, 'Truly I say to you, to the extent that you did it to one of these brothers of Mine, even the least of them, you did it to Me.'" (Matthew 25:37, 40, NAS)

* * * * *

Christian Livingston Seagull

I wanted to learn to fly—to climb, to soar, to spin, to dive with ever-increasing speed and perfection—this was life!

For this unique style of flight, however, spiritual food was an absolute. Morning by morning I perched myself on the Far Cliff of Life and stretched my wings toward the rising sun. After takeoff, I flew slowly and meditatively above the Waters of Time, virtually caressing the wind with my wings. Upward, still upward I climbed, the warm rays of the sun penetrating every curvature of my being. Then I leveled my flight and touched down on the Great Feeding Grounds of my Father in Heaven.

As I looked about me, I saw Him feeding a great multitude who, like myself, were learning to fly. Eager to join in the feast, I folded my wings and partook. I would have remained on those feeding grounds forever had He not nudged me and told me with a glance that simply enjoying the feast wasn't what it was all about! So, lifting one solid wingspan of human frailty and divine strength into the air, I began my descent.

The precise moment I landed, my real flight began! My journey into the heavens was only preparatory for this unique style of flying which inspires and challenges the soul of a woman to glide alongside the soul of her neighbor to bring her to a knowledge of God. I confess my first attempts were nothing more than controlled disasters.

Instead of gliding alongside my neighbor and remaining

at a level of flight consistent with her capacity to learn, I immediately soared to the heights and showed her how she *ought* to fly! With an amazing amount of misplaced confidence, I actually expected her to follow me without even so much as giving her the rudiments of flying. The poor girl hardly knew how to take off, much less soar! Since she was totally lost in all of this futile display of goodness, she thrust my soul from hers with resentment and admiration—a motley but very human mixture of feelings.

This being my first attempt at soul-gliding, I felt altogether useless and discouraged. I wasn't really fashioned for this unique style of flight after all! As I perched on these thoughts, I felt the restraining winds of the grace of God ruffling my feathers. So I left off self-pity and again took up my flight training.

Keeping in mind what I had learned, I glided alongside the soul of my neighbor and immediately fell into a tailspin and dive as I showed her her wretched state in the sight of God. I even named her sins for her one by one! She, too, thrust me from her soul. She secretly hated me, for I had beheld her spiritual nakedness.

Weary from all this conflict and failure, I flew about aimlessly, dreaming of rest. No more victories, no more failures, just pure rest. But once again I felt the restraining winds of the grace of God ruffling my feathers. So I discarded my discouragement and again took up my flight training.

As I glided alongside my neighbor, I fluffed up my feathers of divine strength and hid my feathers of human frailty. For I reasoned, "If I show her God, she will become like Him; whereas if I show her only my sinfulness, my witness will become void!" So saying, I glided alongside her soul. Though she was impressed with my skillful approach, she did not seem to be motivated to do anything about herself! By acting as a robot, I had actually thrown a shadow over the very gospel I proclaimed.

Instead of waiting to be thrown out again, I decided to just leave on my own! I flew off and thought of diving into the Waters of Life and ending it all. For I concluded, "If showing my neighbor God doesn't work, then I have nothing left to offer!" Once again I felt the restraining winds of the grace of God. So again I took up my flight training.

Next, I glided alongside the soul of my neighbor and

155

shared with her my weakness. Though she seemed grateful that I cared enough to identify with her, she was no more moved to action than the others. I left her in anger, for this time she had seen my spiritual nakedness!

I ceased making accusations against myself and began to vent my hostility toward God! Why had He ever sent me on such a mission, anyhow? I was wretchedly inadequate when it came to teaching others how to fly. It was as though everywhere I went, I pulled this huge banner behind me which read, "FAILURE," in every language of the universe! I thought all mankind was looking on. Actually, except for one here and another there, people were much too preoccupied with their own affairs to even notice! For some kind of sanctimonious reasons I didn't understand, I continued to pull my banner behind me anyway, even though doing just this one thing was enough to wear me out!

Then I left the realm of the totally discouraged and became defensive in my attack toward my neighbor. After all, I was a leader! Even though I didn't seem to be making much headway in my flight attempts, why couldn't people acknowledge my leadership and follow me in flight? Once again I felt the restraining winds of the grace of God ruffling my feathers! So I discarded my hatred and pride, and again took up my flight training.

Troubled, I returned to the Great Feeding Grounds. Christ showed me that there was not "one correct way" to reach my neighbor but many ways. I remembered that when He was on earth, He met people where they were—some with firmness, others with compassion, some with anger, others with tears—always addressing each person's genuine needs and thereby not only meeting her needs but underscoring her uniqueness.

The next time I glided alongside the soul of my neighbor, instead of going into an immediate climb or dive, I tried to glide at a level consistent with her needs. Since we were flying together in formation, I was close enough to her to speak, and she was close enough to me to listen.

As we flew, I taught her not as one who has many lifetimes to teach nor as though she had many lifetimes to learn. I yoked together freedom of choice with love; and I neither forced her to fly, nor did I ignore her need to learn. Rather, I constrained her as a sister. I said, "Heaven is a time, and

156

Heaven is a place. I would that we might go there together."

As I taught her the things I knew, she also taught me the things she had learned. As we soared together, I thought, *This is flying indeed!*

This is *serving with love* indeed!

Exercise Courage to Relax in the Midst of Service

We have all exhorted each other through song:

> "Work, for the night is coming, Work thro' the morning hours; Work while the dew is sparkling; Work, 'mid springing flow'rs. Work, when the day grows brighter, Work in the glowing sun; Work, for the night is coming, When man's work is done."

But does that mean that the whole task is ours? That everything depends upon us?

A guest in our home once mentioned that for all the labor a farmer expends to produce a crop—i.e., breaking the ground, disking, fertilizing, planting the seed, cultivating, spraying for insects and weeds, harvesting, etc.—there is still 90% of the energy to be provided. That energy comes from the work of the soil, the wind, the sun, the rain and the energy within the seed itself.

Paul brings out the correct balance of things when he says, "What then is Apollos? And what is Paul? Servants through whom you believed, even as the Lord gave opportunity to each one. I planted, Apollos watered, but God was causing the growth. So then neither the one who plants nor the one who waters is anything, but God who causes the growth" (1 Corinthians 3:5-7, NAS).

The work is God's! We simply put on our gardening clothes and get on with the task at hand—encouraging and helping to bring to harvest God's dreams for the world. What a liberating perspective!

This does not belittle our task. To the contrary, our small plot of ground will turn into a wilderness if we are not faithful with rake and hoe. Certainly, the angels will not trail behind us and pick up the garden tools we have dropped. When we have done *all,* it will only be a small contribution to the Gardener of Life whose labors, power, and beauty could not even have been imagined by us, much less created.

When we view our life and work thusly, we will have time not only to liberate the splendor of God's labors, but to enjoy them! True, life is fleeting. We must keep in mind that which matters most. In concentrating on this truth however, we oftentimes forget to celebrate the temporal while working for the eternal. Thus, consecrated women drive themselves from one task to another and from one place to another unable to look up or to pause.

While women thus bend themselves to their labors, God claps His hands with joy and hurls a thousand paint brushes in the sky and lavishes His love on one passing sunrise. Then He bends low and pours perfume into the tiny flowers. He hands out fleeting smiles to millions of little children, and then climbs back into the heavens to hang up the stars before nightfall. He laughs with delight when He sees how lovely His world is, and He calls it "good." When He calls it "good," He knows that the sky will lose its color, the flowers will die in the heat of the day, the smiles of the little children will turn to tears ere bedtime comes, and the stars will disappear from sight by morning. But it is in His nature to celebrate the temporal while working for the eternal, and He watches His children with their heads pressed down in their tasks and wonders with holy amazement that they do not understand. The next day He begins His temporary tasks all over again. He watches a little chubby hand pick a flower, push it full against his nose, and laugh with glee. And His heart rejoices.

Let us be faithful with rake and hoe to our own little garden plot. As we go forth to our day's labors however, let it not be with the weight of the world on our shoulders, but with a song on our lips and joy in our hearts that we are counted worthy to participate in God's magnificent doings. Then, perchance, we will have time to stop and smell the flowers!

Old Rags and Discarded Garments

Ebed-melech, I pause a moment this morning
to salute you!
I see you in the palace depot
sorting through old rags and discarded garments
with loving hands,
and my heart is strangely stirred.
Oh, what manner of man were you?
Of what was your heart made, Ebed-melech,
that it was so filled with gentleness and compassion?
Were mercy and kindness always written there
or did you have to suffer much to obtain them?
Oh, gentle soul,
the king didn't command you to sort through rags!
He just said, "Pull Jeremiah out before he dies."
Most men would have rushed
to the empty cistern in the prison yard
and thrown down a rope.
But not you!
I think that's why God moved the king to choose you.
Of course, you knew he needed to be saved.
It was you who ran out to the Gate of Benjamin
where the king was holding court
to tell him what evil thing the men had done
and to warn him that Jeremiah would surely die!
But you kept thinking about how much those ropes
would hurt under Jeremiah's armpits!
And you had to head for the place
where the used clothing was kept—
the palace depot for discarded supplies.
Ebed-melech, you who stood on the earth so long ago,
I stand on this same earth centuries later
and salute you!

I can't help but think about all of the
mercy and kindness,
the gentleness and compassion
that we, God's people, have discarded in the palace depot.
Yes, we all live on the palace ground now, Ebed-melech,
for we are all God's children.
But what have we thrown away?
I see some gentle men with your gift of compassion
sorting through the supplies
to have something in their hands
to ease the hurts of others.
Save men? Oh, yes, we must save them!
The King commanded us to!
But I think He had something more in mind
than just throwing down a rope.
I think He would have us gather men with lovingkindness,
placing old rags and discarded garments
over areas where they hurt
as we draw them out of the pit!

(from Jeremiah 38:7-13)

Exercise Courage to

Choose Your Friends

"No one who has a haughty look and an arrogant heart
   will I endure.
My eyes shall be upon the faithful of the land, that
   they may dwell with me;
He who walks in a blameless way is the one who will
   minister to me.
He who practices deceit shall not dwell within my
   house."

(Psalm 101:5-7, NAS)

Being "all things to all men" is the privilege of the spiritually mature. Those of us who have problems to work through would do well to exercise special care about our associates—clinging to some, separating ourselves from others. We do this, not out of a spirit of antagonism, but out of goodwill, recognizing the responsibility that is ours to grow in Christ and choosing responsibly those who would not defeat this goal. I am speaking here of friends and acquaintances for whom we have not been given a direct responsibility by God, such as one carries for his family.

It is not always possible to know why one person affects us for evil and another for good. Two people may have identical faults, and because of other factors we may be able to be friends with one, and at the same time, would be destroyed by our association with the other. Obviously, factors outside the fault are involved—factors which may not even be in the realm of awareness. I say again, it is not hatred but personal weakness which makes close association with some inadvisable. We are not strong enough to bear the sins of the whole world without being damaged.

Guilt experienced when moving out of another's life may not be from God, but from an ill-trained conscience. The excuse-riddled question, "Am I my brother's keeper?" (Genesis 4:9, NAS), does not cancel out the divine directive, "Do not be deceived: 'Bad company corrupts good morals'" (1 Corinthians 15:33, NAS). Only Christ can be the intimate companion of all people. It is our privilege to have the capacity to be intimately involved with a few, and perhaps a shepherdess to some, leaving the "Savior" role with Christ.

When meditating on a parable the Lord once told—the one about the ten virgins who took their lamps and went out to meet the bridegroom—I observed in my reading that the five virgins who would not share their oil were not reprimanded or excluded from the feast. Rather, they were counted wise.

I thought immediately of my friendships—how until the day I was completely broken, I tried desperately to be all things to all people. This was especially true of those in my inner circle of friends! That's good, but there were things I needed to sort out in my thinking—like acknowledging the difference between agape love and friendship love, and coming to grips with the fact that though I owe agape love to all people, I owe my friendship to none. For I have a debt not only to my neighbor, but to myself!

Oh, Lord, give me wisdom in friendship maintenance. If, in any given friendship, the demands made upon me—physically, emotionally, and/or spiritually—become excessive and a drain so that my oil supply is running dangerously low, give me the courage to say, with agape love, "There is not enough oil for both me and you."

Then, having made this decision, carefully, prayerfully, help me to shed false guilt and hasten on my way with "the other five" to the wedding feast! For if there is no longer sufficient oil to carry both my friend and me along the road of life, then it were better that I relinquish my relationship with my friend rather than lose my way in the dark for that one important journey!

Select Friends With Sensitivity

We need to exercise sensitivity in finding our way in the area of friendship. We all live within a limited framework of time, space, and strength. Thus, we are faced with being able to choose only a handful of intimate companions. We may will the good of all, but we cannot be involved with all on the same level that God is simply because we are not God. Even Christ, when He was in the flesh, was limited—clinging to some, blessing others as He passed by. We have the deep privilege and the even deeper responsibility of choosing those with whom we would be close. However, even within this framework, we are greatly limited due to the need for a mutual desire between ourselves and those whom we would befriend.

Fortunately, we can seek the Lord's help and wisdom in all of this. There are no friendships that can match the joy of those He puts together.

Who is she, Lord—
this one You've put into my life?
Why can't I pass her by?
I walk by others, Lord,
without a thought.
They have hopes and dreams
and joys and sorrows
they yearn to share.
Yet, somehow
I can walk by them
without it mattering.
Why does my heart stop to ponder
when I think of her, Lord?
It's as though,
when she comes walking down
the corridor of my heart,
I pause and give
a silent salute!
Then timidly I ask,
with questioning eyes,
not knowing if she sees me,
"Who are you standing there?
What do you carry
in your basket of dreams?
Do you need a friend?
Does your heart hurt?

What makes you what you are?"
And as the questions linger,
a dream begins to form.
Did You put her there for me, Lord?
Should I reach out to her
in friendship born of You?
Or should I pick up
my basket of dreams
and tiptoe quietly by?
Please lead me, Lord.

Exercise Courage to

Remember

In the Kingdom of God, personal failure and success are not two separate garments that we wear but one reversible garment as we sometimes obey, sometimes disobey His commands. Someone asks, "Lois, are you a success or a failure?" And I answer, "Both."

Did you ever dread being around a certain person or place—simply because you didn't want to remember? Maybe some day, when you work through some things, you can handle it. But not now! We all know the feeling. Fortunately, or perhaps unfortunately, the world is big enough so that when we are hurting, we can manage to hide around other people and in other locations. On the other hand, sometimes we can't. That's the way it goes.

It's not the theological answer to all of this that I want us to grasp right now—but simply a feeling. How do you suppose the apostle Peter felt when he heard the first cockcrow after Jesus ascended into Heaven? Do you suppose he ever wondered why Christ tied his denial of Him with the crowing of a cock—a sound from which he could never escape? Why couldn't He have said, "Peter, within a few hours now, you will deny me three times." Then, every time he heard a cock crow it wouldn't have been unbearable. Cocks crow often—like *every day!*

I don't know the answer, and maybe the answer isn't even really important. What is important is that part and parcel of living is the inability to avoid association with people, sounds, and events that trigger the pain of memories we fight to forget. I remember the night our daughter Cindy was run over by a car. I was on my way back home from a choir supper when I passed the scene of the accident. You will understand when I tell you that that choir supper and Cindy's accident were inseparably locked together in my mind—for a long time.

Paul said, "This one thing I do, forgetting those things which are behind, and reaching forth unto those things which are before, I press toward the mark for the prize of the high calling of God in Christ Jesus" (Philippians 3:13, 14). But did Paul really forget? Was it all blocked out so he could get on with it? That hardly seems to be the case. With eloquence he relates, upon more than one occasion, the details surrounding his conversion. With meticulous precision he recounts his sufferings for the Lord—listing not only his deprivations on land and sea, but the number of times various sufferings were inflicted.

Paul "forgot" the past the same way we can "forget our past"—by making the past his servant instead of allowing it to be his master. Whether the past had to do with failure or success was beside the point with Paul because it couldn't be relived. Paul called forth both. The point is that when sharing a past failure would bring home a spiritual point to his listeners and thus glorify God, Paul was free to call upon it as a man is free to call upon his servant—because he had come to grips with it. His "forgetting" was a healthy forgetting, not a blocking out that troubles the inner person and creates a thousand problems within. He was able to come to grips with his past not because it was all victorious. It wasn't. Some of it was shameful. But because he realized that the Lord alone is righteous, that there is forgiveness with Him, and that the Lord could use defeat as well as victory to get the point across to men. Take, for example, Paul's comment to Timothy, "This is a faithful saying, and worthy of all acceptation, that Christ Jesus came into the world to save sinners; of whom I am chief. Howbeit for this cause I obtained mercy, that in me first Jesus Christ might show forth all long-suffering, for a pattern to them which should hereafter believe on him to life everlasting" (1 Timothy 1:15, 16). Paul didn't have to have a clean slate in order to be used. He

166

had to have a slate that was turned over to God—giving God the option of using or not using what was written thereon.

Regarding the subject of righteousness, I recall in Sunday-school class one morning, the teacher asking, "What is the only righteousness?" At first I thought, Christ's and when we are righteous. Some would have pitied me if they could have read my mind. Others would have given the same answer. The teacher's answer was correct; *Christ is the only righteousness.*

We've all heard that "all our righteousnesses are as filthy rags" (Isaiah 64:6). But in some kinds of human personalities those words are translated, "When we aren't righteous, our sins are as filthy rags." It doesn't quite come through that even the best that we have to offer God is polluted with sin and falls far short of His glory. There is so much of self in our highest reachings. The point is that when we see our best as unrighteousness, instead of having the terrible feeling that we were righteous *until* this happened or *until* that happened to ruin our "perfect record," we can have a kind of sanctified "relaxation" in our unrighteousness and press on—"dressed in His righteousness alone." As Paul put it, "I count all things but loss for the excellency of the knowledge of Christ Jesus my Lord: for whom I have suffered the loss of all things, and do count them but dung, that I may win Christ, And be found in him, not having mine own righteousness, which is of the law, but that which is through the faith of Christ, the righteousness which is of God by faith" (Philippians 3:8, 9).

Far from letting His cloak of righteousness be an occasion for carelessness on our part, all the more, out of a spirit of undying gratitude, we ought to grow in Christ. The point is that it is a *growth,* not a falling in and out of righteousness— a growth towards righteousness in our personal unrighteousness. This realization abolishes the anger we experience when we fall and "spoil our record." It establishes us with the human race as sinners saved by grace, sanctified by grace, and glorying only in the true righteousness, which is in Jesus Christ our Lord.

When the cock crows in our lives, as it will, even as it crowed in Peter's life after Christ ascended to Heaven, and we want to avoid persons, things, and places, we can ask God for true healing of mind. This will lead to a healthy forgetting which, in God's hands, may be used to bring Him glory—perhaps even more than those victories which we would like to proclaim from the housetops, supposedly for the nourishing of the saints. The trouble with the saints is that they are like us, and they need our identification as well as our instruction.

So let us be little children in our reaching out to one another and in our sharing of the human predicament. Let us be like grownups in our answers, bringing solutions that are in harmony with the Word of God. Let us, in times of failure as well as in times of victory, lift up Christ!

Exercise Courage to

Get the Victory

Kathy was dying with cancer. One day over the phone she said to a friend of mine, "This dying is so hard. It's all the goodbyes. It's not as if you can comb your hair, straighten the sheets, smile and say, 'Goodbye,' and die. You keep saying, 'Good-bye'—and the dying takes so long."

How like dying to self! This dying is so hard. It's all the goodbyes. You comb your hair, straighten the sheets, smile and say, "I'm all Yours now, Lord!" And you lie down and find the "old self" a bedfellow! Dying takes so long!

In the recent past I suffered a great deal with a displaced sacroiliac. Consequently, I spent a lot of time in the chiropractor's office. Through my suffering, I became aware of another kind of deep suffering—the pain that comes when one's spiritual sacroiliac slips out of place. Until recently, I didn't even know I had a spiritual sacroiliac. One thing I did know about myself was that for most of my life my Christianity wasn't working as it should.

Don't misunderstand me. All my life I loved the Lord, or so I thought, with all my heart, mind, and soul. I grew up in a strong Christian family. My father baptized me in the river located near the country church where he ministered. As I grew up, I did a lot of things that some might consider to be

169

commendable—things like living in a primitive village in a remote area of the world for the sake of Christ, things like teaching the Lisu tribal people how to sing difficult music in their own language, using their own unique system of music notation, and of course, a cappella as we had no pianos out there.

But despite such outward signs of devotion—and deep inner devotions as well, which I don't mean to minimize—I wasn't getting consistent day-by-day victory over the sins of the flesh. And I didn't know why. I agreed with God's moral law in my inner self, but how to obtain it, I knew not.

I battled bitterness. I battled anger. I battled unforgiveness. I battled hatred. Not for the whole world but usually for one person at a time. In fact, my love for the Lord was so intense that I literally fought sin like a tiger. But all I got were tiger wounds in return. Not knowing what else to do, I licked my wounds and went right back into the arena—only to come limping away with more wounds. I didn't understand why I couldn't master sin instead of its mastering me. But, you know, the sad thing is that I didn't worry about it too much for a long time because I observed that others were struggling in the same way. So I took it that mine was a very normal Christian life and that this was the way it would be until I went to Heaven.

In time, however, the pain from living this kind of life became so intense—despite faith, despite good works, despite Bible reading, despite fasting, despite prayer, despite all my striving. I was driven to find the answer to my personal lack of victory or to die trying.

During this period of my life I closed all the books on my bookshelves—books that had "promised" to give the answers—and buried myself in the Word of God and in the personal ministry of Christ to me through His Word. He didn't say anything to me He hadn't already said. He doesn't, you know. But as I saturated my mind with His Word and reached out to Him and He to me, *He met me* at the level of my despair and gave me a concept I could grasp.

Slowly I began to understand that I had not only a physical sacroiliac but a spiritual sacroiliac as well, and that spiritual sacroiliac could be likened to the first two commandments, "You shall love the Lord your God with all your heart, and with all your soul, and with all your mind," and "You shall love your neighbor as yourself" (Matthew. 22:37, 39 NAS). I began to realize that my bitterness, my anger, my unforgiveness, etc., were merely symptoms of a displaced spiritual sacroiliac.

Now this was a revolutionary concept to me. Because, you see, all my life I was convinced that Christ *was first,* but being human I naturally had some sins I needed to overcome. I didn't understand that the presence of sin in my life was a clear indication that Christ *was not first* in some area of my life—all of my feelings and declarations not withstanding. Neither did I understand that my focusing in on my sin, instead of my spiritual displacement with God and my brother, was about as foolish as it would have been for me to have focused on my pain instead of going to my chiropractor when my physical sacroiliac slipped out of place.

In this day of great emphasis on relational theology, it is imperative that we remember that Christianity is first *positional* and then *relational.* Christ said that if we love anyone or anything more than we love Him, we cannot be His disciples. It took me nearly fifty years to understand that "cannot" means *"cannot."* We simply cannot do it! We can pray over our sins from morning till night, repent seventy times seven, read our Bibles all day long, fast, agonize, do good works, fast, pray again, and possess the Holy Spirit because of our baptism into Christ. But until we go back to the first and second Commandments, and with a humble and contrite heart, ask our heavenly Father who or what we have placed above Him, or what person we have positioned higher or lower than ourselves, we cannot be released from our bitterness, our anger, etc., nor from the terrible pain and immobilization that displacement always brings. Incidentally, depression may sometimes be overcome by asking the same questions.

I want to share with you just one example of how this works. Here is a woman who has a dream—a magnificent dream for the glory of God. Now this woman believes with all of her heart that Christ is first in her life. However, without her conscious awareness, her dream slips into first place. She begins to notice that she is having conflicts in her relationships with others, but she doesn't connect her problems with the mispositioning of her dream. As her spiritual sacroiliac slips still further out of place, anything or anyone who stands in the way of her dream becomes an immediate target for her frustration—which is sometimes dressed in anger, sometimes in hatred, sometimes in jealousy, and so forth. Now this woman, because of her sincere devotion to Christ, may concentrate on getting rid of her anger, hatred, and jealousy from morning till night. But until she repositions her dream, she will be locked into spiritual problems. For every sin against another is always a second offense. We always sin against God first.

Taking up our crosses daily, then, is not fighting sin like a tiger, as I did most of my life, but simply acknowledging who or what is dearer to us than God, and releasing it to Him. When the Great Physician puts our spiritual sacroiliac back in place, our sins of the flesh will vanish as the morning dew.

Whenever I went into my chiropractor's office with a displaced sacroiliac, he never scolded me. He always showed deep compassion. He explained to me why I was having problems. Then he gave me the needed adjustment.

It occurs to me this is how we ought to be ministering to one another. So many who truly love the Lord are caught up in sin's grip without even understanding the dynamics of what is going on. Consequently, they live lives of quiet despair. We need to reach out to these people with compassion and skill—the same kind of compassion and skill my chiropractor always extended to me when I walked into his office bent over with pain.

Happiness Is Going Home

"There's no place like home...."

She threw her arms around the Lion's neck and kissed him, patting his big head tenderly. Then she kissed the Tin Woodman, who was weeping in a way most dangerous to his joints. But she hugged the soft, stuffed body of the Scarecrow in her arms instead of kissing his painted face, and found she was crying herself at this sorrowful parting from her loving comrades....

Dorothy now took Toto up solemnly in her arms, and having said one last good-bye she clapped the heels of her shoes together three times, saying,

"Take me home to Aunt Em!"

Instantly she was whirling through the air so swiftly that all she could see or feel was the wind whistling past her ears.

The Silver Shoes took but three steps, and then she stopped so suddenly that she rolled over upon the grass several times before she knew where she was.

At length, however, she sat up and looked about her.

"Good gracious!" she cried.

For she was sitting on the broad Kansas prairie....

Home Again

Aunt Em had just come out of the house to water the cabbages when she looked up and saw Dorothy running toward her.

"My darling child!" she cried, folding the little girl in her arms and covering her face with kisses. "Where in the world did you come from?"

173

"From the Land of Oz," said Dorothy gravely. "And here is Toto, too. And, oh, Aunt Em! I'm so glad to be at home again!"

* * * * *

When it's time for you and me to go Home,
we can't cling to anyone or anything but Christ.

My beloved husband grew up in China, the son of missionary parents. He returned to the States to receive his high-school education and then entered Bible College. In 1949, shortly before the Communist take-over in China, he returned to the mission field in order to work together with his family for the ongoing of Christ's kingdom in that part of the world. I want to share with you, in LaVerne's own words, the following account:

"In the summer of 1950, I was preaching and teaching in N'Mai Hka Valley of the upper Irrawaddy River, near where Burma, China, and Tibet meet, when a terrible earthquake hit the entire region. It was an earthquake of very great intensity (about 8.0 on the Richter scale) which hit much of the eastern Himalayan Mountains of Asia.

"In the darkness of the night, suddenly the mountains started shaking, with crashing roars in the blackness which sounded as though the mountains were falling into the canyons below. A group of us who had gathered in a bamboo house for evening singing and Bible study could not stand up because of the terrific shaking of the house and the mountains around, but we had to hold the pillars of the house, or trees outside for some support. We feared that the entire village might slide into the deep canyon thousands of feet below. As the intense shaking continued for about thirty minutes and the booming, roaring sound came from over the western mountains, we wondered whether the world was coming to an end. It sounded as though the mountains were splitting.

"The quakes gradually subsided, but came at short intervals for about twelve hours. When the day dawned, we were surprised to see the mountains still standing normally around us, even though great cracks in the earth, and thousands of landslides, had changed the surfaces of the mountains.

"During this time, at another village, we heard that non-Christians who had heard the Christians teaching about the end of the world, and the coming of Christ, had thought that the time had surely come. During the crashing of the earthquake, the non-Christians had hurried to the Christians, and had hung onto the Christians saying, 'If you're going to Heaven now, we want to go too!' And so they clung to the Christians with their arms around them."

What a typical reaction to such a frightening experience! The non-Christians turned to the Christians to be saved by association. Can't you just picture this—during a twelve hour ordeal, these non-Christians held onto the Christians and wanted to go to Heaven with them.

The truth is, my friends, that Christ is the only One to whom we can cling. He is the One who brings happiness. He is our salvation—He is our solid rock!

Epilogue

> Now it was the Sabbath on that day. Therefore the Jews were saying to him who was cured, "It is the Sabbath, and it is not permissible for you to carry your pallet." But he answered them, "He who made me well was the one who said to me, 'Take up your pallet and walk.'" They asked him, "Who is the man who said to you, 'Take up your pallet, and walk'?" But he who was healed did not know who it was; for Jesus had slipped away while there was a crowd in that place.
>
> (John 5:9-13, NAS)

When Jesus finds the need, for reasons of His own, to slip away unnoticed into the crowd, that's one thing. But when He slips away into the crowd following a healing because some person or some teaching is taking the credit, it's one of the saddest things that ever happens. Because people really need to know that it's Jesus who is healing them.

Before you lay this book down, and remember I told you that I would be honest with you, I want to be certain that you understand that if any line or thought I have expressed has been used to bring some measure of healing to your life, it was really Jesus who was reaching out to you in love and healing you. I am only a small instrument in *His* hands, and it is *His* hands that bring healing.

Our three companions have reminded us that as we travel on life's journey we need to seek God's help in making friends with our minds, enlarging our hearts in all situations, and exercising courage to remain faithful. We need to be careful that we don't stop two blocks from happiness, but continue on to our Heavenly Home.

Thank you for journeying along with me on the yellow brick road to the City of God. Perhaps we will meet again. I love you.

Lois E. Morse